A LEAP OF FAITH

Celebrating 50 Years of the Durham Rescue Mission

ANDREA HIGGINS

FAITHFUL LIFE
Publishers

Printed in the United States of America

Foreword

Nothing occurs outside the will and purpose of God. If God wants something to happen, nothing can stop it.

One of the things that is awesome to witness on this earth is the power of God displayed in a world that doesn't believe He exists. When you examine the lives of Ernie and Gail Mills and the history of the Durham Rescue Mission, God's power is obvious throughout. There is no other explanation. From God planting a desire in Ernie more than 50 years ago to help the addicted beginning in a single house in Durham, NC, to the Durham Rescue Mission campuses and the many other support facilities in the Raleigh-Durham area that stand today, what you see is one miracle of God after another.

However, God's greatest miracles are the thousands of lives He's changed through the Durham Rescue Mission ministry. Broken people from all walks of life come to the Durham Rescue Mission— most at the end of their rope. They enter hopeless and most walk out with a new life through the power of Jesus Christ. If you enjoy witnessing God's power as much as I do, I know you will enjoy reading this book.

—Gary Hahn
Retired Radio Play-by-Play Announcer, NC State Athletics, Raleigh, NC

Acknowledgments

It's not just because he founded a homeless mission that Rev. Ernie Mills can make you feel at home wherever you are. His soft Southern drawl carries that warm, melodic cadence that instantly puts the listener at ease. Whether he's wearing a suit or a plaid shirt, his humility and sincerity are equally disarming and charming.

This preacher's sermons are rich tapestries woven with threads of Scripture and the vibrant colors of his own rural experiences. He tells stories of tilling the soil, tending crops, patching tobacco barn roofs, seamlessly tying these earthy experiences to biblical parables and teachings. His words resonate deeply because they are born from an early life lived close to the land, a life that mirrors the simplicity and depth of the biblical stories he shares.

His hands gesture gently as he speaks, painting vivid pictures of faith, struggle, and redemption. Each story he tells is a lesson, drawn from the pages of the Bible and illustrated with the rich detail of his own home-spun anecdotes. He talks about the patience needed to wait for a crop to grow, paralleling it with the patience we must have for God's timing. He speaks of the literal and figurative storms that threatened what he tried to grow, likening them to the trials and tribulations we all face in life.

His congregation hangs on his every word, feeling the weight and warmth of his message in their hearts. They leave the service not just with a deeper understanding of the Scripture, but with a sense of connection to a simpler, more profound way of living and believing.

I remember the second time I spoke with him. He was pointing at me with one of those characteristic hand gestures.

"That story had heart!" he exclaimed. He and wife Gail invited me to their office at the Durham Rescue Mission. I didn't know why, only that I'd recently written a freelance article for the Raleigh News & Observer about volunteers adopting rooms to decorate at the Good Samaritan Inn, the Mission's women's shelter. It was a tiny feature, so I wondered if they wanted another article about something else.

"People have written about us for a long time, but that story had heart," Ernie repeated. I smiled and was so moved he liked it. It's always my goal to get to the heart of a story, so it meant a lot coming from the preacher known for his heartfelt storytelling.

It turned out, he wanted a whole book, which wasn't on my bingo card that day. With two small kids, one of whom is disabled, I just wasn't sure I could do it. Gail nodded her head and said they prayed about it, and knew I was the person to do it. Even if I tried to protest, for those of you with the privilege to know Ernie Mills, you know he can be convincing, and the two of them are a force of faith. Soon enough, we were talking regularly, and they regaled me with some of the most outlandish and heartwarming stories I'd ever heard.

Every week, it seemed Ernie would have me laughing out loud about some improbable situation that you couldn't make up. The unforgettable characters with fitting and colorful names soon filled the pages of the book. "A Step of Faith: The History of the Durham Rescue Mission," was published in 2006 for the Mission to use in their ministry.

Unbeknownst to me, Gail and Ernie shared the proofs with long-time Mission supporter Harold Strawbridge, owner of Strawbridge Studios, Inc. He loved it so much; he printed 20,000 copies for the Mission at his publishing company. I wish I'd had the chance to meet him and thank him personally. He passed away in 2019. People I encounter through the Mission sometimes tell me they re-read the book, and they'll never know how much that means.

Fast forward, and suddenly the Mission was looking forward to its 50th anniversary coming up in 2024. This time when they called, I volunteered to do the next "chapter" without hesitation, despite a demanding work and homelife schedule. The first book is still my favorite thing I ever wrote. The stories for this second book did not disappoint.

This time, I got to spend about an hour each week chatting with the then-new Mission CEO Rob Tart. While in some ways he couldn't be more different than Ernie Mills, Rob Tart has a way of sharing a big vision matched only by his enormous compassion and dedication to helping others.

All the Mission leaders have impacted countless lives in profound ways, including mine.

- So, to Rob Tart and those who carry the torch of the Mission, your commitment to serving the community is inspiring.

- To Executive Administrative Assistant Elisabeth Todd, who helped me connect with Rob Tart and Mission clients when I needed to, thank you for always being available to help.

- To David Rayle, whose attention to detail in the layout of the book is just amazing, thank you for your tireless help and expertise.

- To the donors like Phil Clegg, whose generosity and heartfelt stories fuel the Mission's work, your contributions make a tangible difference in the lives of those in need.

- To the clients who shared their truly incredible stories of struggle, resilience, and redemption, thank you for trusting me with your experiences. It has been an amazing journey to know you.

Finally, to my kids, Alexandra and Andrew, thank you for never complaining when I chose to spend weekends at the computer instead of adventuring with you. Thank you, Alex, for listening and sharing your storyteller opinions until a chapter "sang." And thank you to my husband, Jerry, for clearing the calendar so my weekends were for interviews and churning out chapters. Thank you for your eagle eye and editing skills, helping me keep word count to a reasonable level, and everything you did to keep the house from falling down while I finished it.

I am so grateful and honored to be part of this project.

—Andrea Higgins

TABLE OF
Contents

Introduction

Pastor's Quarter 'Down Payment' Returned: Debt Paid in Full

I t was 1978 and a young pastor—who didn't have two nickels to rub together, as the saying goes—just dropped a quarter into a crack in the weathered brick wall of the old church where he was trying to move the Durham Rescue Mission.

His faith was full. His wallet, not so much.

While a quarter couldn't buy a loaf of bread back then, if you had two, you "might could," as the locals are prone to say in Durham, North Carolina. Durham was known as a banking and tobacco center early on. It gained its nickname as the Bull City from Bull Durham tobacco in the late 1800s, the namesake of the iconic baseball movie, and home to the famous minor league baseball team, the Durham Bulls.

Durham is also known as the City of Medicine, anchored by the renowned Duke University Hospital and hundreds of medical companies. It is home to the cutting-edge global technology innovation center, Research Triangle Park, named for its proximity to the Raleigh-Durham-Chapel Hill "Triangle" area and other top universities.

Juxtaposed to frequent "best of" magazine rankings—as home the elite Duke University campus and its storied Blue Devils teams and Tobacco Road sporting rivalries, world-class museums, colorful performing and visual arts attractions, celebrated revitalization efforts like the upscale American Tobacco campus, and a reputation as a fashionable foodie and brewery destination—is the other side of Durham.

The 1957 Royal Ice Cream Sit-in to protest Durham's segregation and Jim Crow history inspired other more famous protests across the southeast during the Civil Rights Movement. Racial tensions and economic disparities were perhaps most strikingly illustrated as the Durham Freeway and urban sprawl cut through the very heart of Durham's own "Black Wall Street" district in the 1960s and 1970s. Underfunded and poor public-school performance, drug and gang problems, and rising costs due to gentrification that worsen affordable housing challenges persist.

∽

Bread of Life—Not Just Sandwiches

∽

Back in 1974, that young pastor, Ernest "Ernie" Mills, came to Durham to help homeless alcoholics and addicts, a population on the rise with the influx of cocaine and crime in the community.

As he stood behind that old church a few years later, he sure could have used a loaf of bread to help feed the hungry men staying at the Mission.

The trouble was, he didn't just want to serve sandwiches to homeless alcoholics. He wanted to nourish hopeless men's souls with spiritual manna—to do what God called him to—share the "bread of life."

They needed more than a meal. No matter how hard quarters were to come by in those days, clients at the Mission needed to learn to love themselves and others through a relationship with Jesus Christ to satisfy their souls, Mills believed with all his heart.

Between the Pastor, the Wall and God

So, he knelt down at the back of the church where he'd dropped that quarter as an offering made out of his poverty. He couldn't imagine how he'd get what he needed to move the Mission forward, let alone the next meal. With all that uncertainty, alone, he prayed.

"Lord, this is my down payment. If you want us to have this, you've got to come up with the rest," he prayed aloud in his soft Southern accent.

Ernie Mills at the place where he put the quarter in as a down payment on the old church building

The moving story is the touchstone moment that became the hallmark for touching hearts through 50 years of Rev. Mills' ministry. It's a story so often told and retold, it's literally and figuratively part of the Mission's foundation.

Two Sides of the Same Coin

So, Mission Chief Operating Officer Rob Tart could hardly pass up the chance to joke with Mills about how sometimes the details in the story changed in the many retellings. In 2021, as Mills was about to pass the torch to Tart to lead the Mission, Tart had a surprise for his longtime mentor and friend at the annual gala.

"Tell me this. Was it a half dollar, a silver dollar or a quarter you dropped behind that wall, because I've heard all three," Tart rapidly grilled Mills as they stood on the Gala stage that night.

Shrugging with a good-natured grin, Mills couldn't lie, but he was fairly certain it wasn't a silver dollar he dropped back there.

"Uh, I don't know whether it was a quarter or a fifty-cent piece. I have said both," he admitted sheepishly. "It was about this round," Mills shook with laughter as he touched his forefinger and thumb together in a circle. Mills flashed a wide grin to the crowd, who laughed right along with him.

Before taking the reins in 2021, Tart spent 26 years working alongside Mills and building the Mission far beyond whatever anyone envisioned in 1974 when Mills and his wife, Gail, started it. With the handoff in 2021, husband-and-wife founders stepped into a fundraising role as Tart took charge.

Ernie Mills exchanges a Bible with Rob Tart symbolizing the passing of the Durham Rescue Mission leadership to Tart. Programs will change but God's Word will not.

As different as they appear, the two men are two sides of the same coin when it comes to their relentless dedication to the Mission. Like-minded about the importance of the Mission and their own roles in it, the two share a similar dry wit and good humor along with their deep passion for the Mission.

Standing side-by-side, though, their different styles stood in stark contrast. Mills, with a ready and sometimes mischievous smile, is outspoken and gregarious with a flair for animated storytelling and energetic arm gestures. By contrast, Tart's steady presence, tall frame and understated, almost reserved demeanor, offers a calm, friendly reassurance.

So, as Tart pursued his questioning of Mills about that quarter he dropped inside the church walls, the smile he'd been trying to hide broke through.

"Do you know what year that quarter was?" Tart asked Mills like a lawyer interrogating a witness on the stand.

"No," replied Mills, his eyes wide with surprise at that question.

"I know what year it was!" Tart replied. "Because we found it!"

"Wait—so you found it?" asked a stunned Gail Mills, who co-ran the Mission all those years.

"I found it," exclaimed Tart.

"What year was it?" interjected Mills amid the murmurs of surprise and delight.

"1967," Tart replied, asking for his team, waiting in the wings, to bring forward the rediscovered quarter, now framed for posterity.

Giving New Meaning to Penny (or Quarter) Pinching

As Tart presented the plaque, his laughter, excitement, and joking gave way to the depth of emotion he feels for the Mission, and his long-time friend—and how much those oft-told stories affected and shaped his life. Holding back those strong emotions, he began to read the plaque.

"It says... this is quoted from your book! Okay? And you said quarter in your book, by the way. It says, 'One day, I walked behind the church building and I saw a little crack in the brickwork. I reached in my pocket and pulled out a quarter. I walked up to that loose brick, stuck a quarter in the crack. As it fell down the interior wall, I knelt down and said, Lord...'" I can't say it," Tart trailed off, his voice choked with emotion.

So moved in that moment by the beloved story, that's all Tart could get though as he handed the microphone to Mike Walker, head of Mission maintenance, who helped fish out the quarter, to read the prayer Ernie Mills made that day he dropped the quarter in the crack in the wall—the day one small quarter and a giant faith began a whole new life for the Mission.

As the applause rose, Tart regained his composure and joyfully seized the microphone again.

"Hold on! Hold on! I'm not done yet," he smiled. "So... it also says, 'The actual quarter that Ernie Mills used,' and I'm not gonna go through all this, but we've also got a verse on there. James 5:16. The effectual fervent prayer of a righteous man availeth much.'"

Everyone looked at the plaque in awe, and then Tart's humor and easy teasing of his mentor returned.

"I want you to look at this quarter! The thing is bent in! Now, I've heard of people pinching a quarter now, but brother, what'd you do?" And the crowd laughed and cried along.

'You Need to Get That Quarter.'

The story of recovering the famous quarter is now part of Mission lore, too, as it started a new chapter under Tart's leadership. The idea came from Tart's wife, Lynda, who wondered out loud about how hard it would be to recover that iconic quarter from behind the brick wall as the team was discussing plans for the 2021 gala and handoff.

"I heard that story so many times, I know exactly where that quarter is," Tart said. "You need to get that quarter," was his wife's simple reply.

A secret sleuthing operation started behind the wall. It was so secret, when Walker enlisted the help of two clients to chip away at the bricks for some unspecified repairs he said they needed, he didn't tell them about the quarter. Then, he asked if they found anything behind the wall.

"Uh, no, not really—oh, I did find this quarter," said one, pulling the corroded coin casually from his pocket.

They promptly set about getting it framed for the gala.

What the Mission has done over the five decades since Ernie Mills dropped that quarter as a down payment is not a calculation with a quantifiable answer. The stories shared here illustrate how far that quarter multiplied like loaves and fishes through two quarters of a century since.

CHAPTER
One

A New Chapter. A New Chaplain.

When Rob Tart arrived in 1995, the Durham Rescue Mission had the main church building and a collection of small row houses on the block nearby. Today, modern dormitories stand sentinel around the old church—in place of and in stark contrast to—those rundown shacks that served the Mission's humble beginnings.

"Every piece of ground they owned was covered in gravel—and the biggest wood pile you ever want to see," Tart said. The wood was for the pot belly stoves in the old houses where Mission clients stayed, and it fed the ancient wood-fired water stove heater that rumbled, rattled, and crackled to warm clients and staff in the drafty church back in the day.

That wood pile grew even larger after 1996's Hurricane Fran, which made landfall in North Carolina and tore a path of destruction from the coast to the Piedmont. People hauled in loads of chopped wood from a virtual forest of trees now strewn across the landscape.

As Tart talks about how the Mission buildings—and the vision for its future—grew, too, over the years, the memories are tightly intertwined with those of his own family and of founders, Ernie and Gail Mills.

Different Backgrounds Led to Same Place

Hired as Mission chaplain, Tart first moved into one of those old houses on North Holman Street with his wife, Lynda, and eight-month-old daughter Katie, the first of their six children.

"When we first came, I was a little bit leery," admits Lynda.

"A mom doesn't really want to take her family amidst alcoholics and drug dealers. You want your kids to go out and play in the yard. You're a protective mom," she said.

She has to smile when she looks back now on how many of those former drug dealers and alcoholics—whose lives were changed by the Mission—became like trusted, even beloved, protective family members, to her, her husband, and all six of her children who grew up among them.

For Tart, being chaplain was definitely his passion, but he didn't shy away from helping with other needs at the mission besides counseling.

"Somewhere along the way, they gave me more responsibility and called me Director," Tart said, adding it was a bit of a confusing title, because Mills was Executive Director. Eventually, he became Chief Operating Officer, and in 2021, Mills handed the reins to Tart as Chief Executive Officer of the Mission.

In some ways, Tart couldn't be more different than founder Ernie Mills. Tart's stoic, quiet, analytical nature juxtaposed to Mills' animated, even feverish enthusiasm may make the two men seem very different on the surface. But along with sharing a deep faith and passion for helping the homeless, they also seem to have the same boundless energy, good humor—and sense of fun that propels the Mission forward.

Tart paused, thinking about Ernie and Gail Mills and how it all started—and how his mentor likes to spin a yarn. Tart enjoys ribbing Ernie about that quality as much as he does listening to the master storyteller preach and share his endearing and inspiring testimony.

"It's interesting sometimes how the background facts kind of change when he tells it the next time," Tart chuckles. But then he quickly becomes thoughtful and serious.

"You know, I've heard their stories so many times. People will ask how Gail ever got mixed up with Ernie, and Ernie will say she came stumbling in with the other alcoholics. She puts up with it," Tart says matter-of-factly about the inseparable pair.

'They're just great people.'

"But, when they started, there were 12 beds and no heat. They lived in the parsonage and there were holes in the walls. It was infested with insects. I've just heard those stories and I've just come to believe—they're great people," Tart said simply.

"They'd be the first ones to tell you it was God's doing," Tart said. "But He did it through them."

As witness for nearly three decades to what the Ernie and Gail Mills did to build the Mission and help others, Tart reaffirms: "They're just great people."

The two men are different, no doubt. Ernie Mills was raised by a loving but alcoholic father, who pleaded with his son on his deathbed to stay away from alcohol. Tart never had an addiction, nor family members with addiction problems. What he had was a strong interest in biblical counseling.

"For people to understand, the Mission is kind of like a small Bible institute. The Mills and the Mission believe in the sufficiency of scripture. We don't mix secular ideas into our plan to help people." Tart explained.

His Mission Field Wasn't as Far Afield as Planned

How Rob Tart ended up at the Mission surprised even him at the time.

He was prepared and truly believed God called him to foreign missions as a young man. He felt it so strongly, he gave up a good job overseas to head back home and follow the call he was sure meant him for the foreign mission field.

The funny thing was, the journey he thought would take him to the foreign mission field kept leading him back to the state where he was born. Every step of faith was a message reinforced that his skills were needed on the home front where he was serving, feeding the hungry, counseling wounded souls, housing the homeless.

After all, with no place to call home, the homeless clients at the Durham Rescue Mission were wanderers who became all but strangers—foreigners if you will—to their communities, families and even to themselves. Eventually, the farther away from foreign missions as a goal he got, the deeper his roots—and the greater his vision grew for how to serve right here.

Sometimes the path that led clients to homelessness was through addiction, sometimes poor decisions, sometimes circumstances. Tart realized he was called to walk alongside and help equip those homeless souls here, and that God was calling him all along to the Durham Rescue Mission as his mission field.

A Mind for Business and Seeing the Big Picture

Tart was born in the agricultural, rural Harnett County, North Carolina. He had a peripatetic childhood because his dad's job for the military moved the family around a lot—first moving to the Spring Lake, North Carolina area in Cumberland County, then Myrtle Beach, South Carolina and on to Enterprise, Alabama, where he attended high school.

In 1983, Tart was finishing high school and working as an assistant manager at McDonald's. He worked at McDonald's for one year after High School. He was not sure what he wanted to do with his life, so he signed up and even took the physical to join the Air Force. But then his mom asked him to check out an exciting new job opportunity through the Army & Air Force Exchange Service (AAFES) where his dad worked.

The AAFES runs the military Post Exchange (PX) and just signed a deal to open Burger Kings on military bases. Tart was soon hired to manage a new Burger King on base in Fort Knox, Kentucky, and the Air Force released him for the promising business opportunity. After three years, he was asked to move to Aschaffenburg, West Germany to manage a Burger King for the PX on base there.

With a strong Christian upbringing, while in Germany, Tart found not one, but two churches, where he attended alongside both American and German missionaries.

"I was in church three or four times a day every Sunday. I met a lot of missionaries, and went to a lot of conferences with missionaries. I just felt, well maybe this is why the Lord sent me to Germany, to introduce me to foreign missions," Tart said.

He asked the missionary pastor he knew how to know if the Lord was calling him to foreign missions.

"I don't think you can know, but it won't hurt you to go study the Bible for four years," the pastor replied.

Tart made up his mind, and resigned his managerial position and enrolled in Bob Jones University in 1989 with a goal of foreign missions.

As an "older" 24-year-old freshman, he met Lynda Elmer, who was a senior getting her degree in home economics. He'd seen her around

Rob and Lynda Tart on Bob Jones University's Graduation Day in May of 1995. Rob is holding their first child Katie.

campus, and met her through a mutual friend who invited him to join them at lunch. After lunch, he smoothly picked up Lynda's bookbag and offered to carry it to her next class, Lynda recalls.

Lynda's dad and all his brothers attended Bob Jones. When Lynda introduced her fiancé, Tart readily won over her conservative dad. He was impressed the young student had already paid off his truck, for one thing, Lynda laughed. With her dad's approval, the couple married as Tart was completing his undergraduate degree in 1993 and embarking on his master's degree in Religious Education.

He finished his master's in 1995, and promptly took his impressive credentials to the Bob Jones Foreign Missions Board, which just as promptly turned down his application.

Tart chalks it up to his being raised a Free Will Baptist, and the board not approving of that, despite his two degrees from their own prestigious university. Whatever their reasons, it was a blow to his long-held belief and plan that he should be a foreign missionary.

Disappointed, he spoke with his pastor that he knew since he was ten years old. His pastor happened to be a long-time supporter of the Durham Rescue Mission.

From Chaplain to Chief 'Cook & Bottle Washer'

Victory & Thrift

Ernie Mills hired Tart on as chaplain at the Mission in 1995.

About two years before Tart arrived, the Mission started a Women's Division in two of the homes, which housed four women and three children. How it would grow would astound even Ernie Mills, who once noted, "My vision wasn't big enough," for what God intended for it. The men's housing averaged about 30–40 in warmer months, and up to 70 in winter when temperatures plunged.

After Tart arrived, the Mission began its highly successful Victory Program, which includes six months of full-day biblical classroom studies, followed by six months of work experience that Tart calls part of their "therapy." Tart taught in the program since its inception.

"Generally, the people aren't resistant. They're probably new and naïve and don't know what they've gotten themselves into," he smiled. To enroll in the Victory Program, clients must be at the mission at least three weeks first.

When the Lord gives up on us, we'll have the liberty to give up on others.

Rob Tart, CEO, Durham Rescue Mission

"We want them to get an idea of who we are and what we do. They've often been to other places, secular shelters. We meet with them individually and explain the program," Tart said.

Tart makes sure clients understand there's no "secret sauce," really, but what differentiates it from other programs are the personal responsibilities and practical opportunities built on a period of spiritual training with a goal to help the individual develop a personal relationship with Jesus Christ.

"We believe you have to learn how to create relationships. And that begins with your own relationship with Jesus Christ," Tart said.

"The second thing that's a little different, is the doctrine of vocation—the calling that everybody has. So often, men lose hope and direction because they feel like there is no overall call for them to do. They learn that God has a calling for their life and relationships. It's very inspiring and motivating," Tart said of how the program helps them tie it all together.

In 2001, the Mission started its sister non-profit organization, Temps to the Rescue, which dovetailed with the Victory Program, helping clients find job opportunities in the community.

Growing Family. Growing Mission. Growing Pains

Before he knew it, three more children came along, Brittany, Heidi, and then Alexander in 2002. Meanwhile, the Mission grew dramatically.

He'd been there seven years when, in 2002, the Mission acquired the old Durham Inn motel off of Interstate 85 at East Knox Street. The Mission dubbed it the Good Samaritan Inn, with plans to use for its women, children, and family division.

Ultimately, the Inn exceeded expectations. It went on to house and helps train and support more than 100 women, children, and families—a far cry from the four women and three children the Mission could house in two small homes when they started their Women's Division a couple years before Tart arrived. However, getting it off the ground created a lot of stress on staff at the time, Tart said.

"I think that was a rough season in the Mission's history. It took us over three years to get it opened in 2005. It was difficult. Nothing was working. People were making promises and couldn't fulfill them," Tart recalled.

Thrift Stores and Storing up 'Treasure'

The following year, in 2006, at Tart's encouragement, the Mission opened its first Thrift Store, creating an income stream to make planning and operating a little more comfortable. The more income they had, the more clients the Mission could serve. Gail Mills chose the name for the first store, "Rescued Treasures."

Ernie wasn't opposed to opening thrift stores, necessarily, but in his early days of working in ministry, "he'd about run his legs off" working for a mission thrift store, and it was a deep-rooted memory of physical pain that made him not as enthusiastic as he might have been.

Tart said: "I remember talking to Pastor Neil Wilcox, his former boss, when preacher Mills initially didn't want to get a thrift store. Rev. Wilcox, said, 'Rob, you gotta understand, I had him working.'" It's a story Ernie tells, too, about his early days in mission life. He jokes about it mostly, but the pain was real.

Once the income started coming in, and the training opportunities for clients started multiplying, Ernie enthusiastically supported the benefits. Plus, he didn't have to carry all the heavy items, he laughed.

"Rob was hired as a counselor, but very quickly, Ernie saw he had the ability to manage people," Gail said.

Ernie agreed, and more importantly, he said, "Rob had the ability to build a team. He knew how to create teamwork."

"Rob is a wonderful manager," agreed Gail. "He works well with people, but he is very unassuming. He always looked to Ernie for leadership, and would run things by him," Gail said. "We are very excited at ideas that Rob has come up with and that now other people

The opening of the Durham Rescue Mission's third store in December 2012. These are the first employees of the store with store manager Rich Carr (far right).

are seeing his leadership ability," she said, noting he's been asked to advise other missions about building successful thrift stores, and to serve on several boards for other rescue missions and ministries that work with rescue missions.

"He's got confidence in what the Lord can do," she said. "It builds confidence in others."

Contrasting the two leaders, Gail said: "Ernie is a visionary. Ernie just looks at the big picture. In five minutes, he could blurt out more than the staff could accomplish in six months. Rob is an organizer. He's more of a details person, and he can get those things organized and get them going."

"But Rob was more of a visionary about our Thrift Stores way before I saw that vision," Ernie replied. "To be honest, I gave Rob a little stiff arm sometimes. It wasn't really the direction I wanted to go into. But it really helped give stability to the Mission. We're able to give job training, and the merchandise could be sold to get money to pay the salaries," Ernie said. "Truly, Rob was right and I was wrong. The Mission is much better today because of him."

"We like to say, if you're clothes are no longer becoming to you, we hope they'll be coming to us," Ernie chuckled, sharing his trademark home-spun wit.

The second store followed in 2009, just three years after the first one opened. That the second store opened on the heels of the housing-crisis fueled economic crash and amid what came to be known as "The Great Recession" is another one of those little multiplied miracles that seem to follow the Mission. The good news, you see, Tart observed, was thrift stores do better in a down economy. That meant the Mission could help more people left out by the economic downturn.

For the opening of the second store, this time Tart picked the name, The Bargain Center. But he later conceded, as much as he didn't think people understood Rescued Treasures had anything to do with the work that was going on at the Mission or that it was a biblical play on words, he later realized the Bargain Center didn't make people think of the Mission, either. Eventually, when they opened more stores, he would settle on The Durham Rescue Mission Thrift Stores for all the stores to be called as they grew.

"As we look back, we see just about every time we expanded, we would opened a Thrift Store and the income that it generated helped pay that operating cost for that new facility," Gail said. "We have five new buildings, and we have five Thrift Stores."

Beyond financial stability, though, the Thrift Stores build confidence in the clients, Gail said.

"Some had never been able to get a job. It helps them feel better about themselves and their ability. We see the Thrift Stores as a springboard to get a job.

A Family Mission: 'Moving in the Same Direction'

From scouting to planning to purchasing the locations, the thrift stores were Tart's baby, no doubt, but they were far from the only milestones he celebrated.

In 2009, the same year as the second store, along came Tart's daughter, Sophie. Son Isaac was born in 2013, the same year firstborn, Katie, graduated high school. He had six kids now, along with the Mission's future to nurture.

Lynda, with her home economics degree, would help the women clients as much as she could, driving them to the grocery store, teaching women in the Women's Division about meal management and other skills, all the while home schooling her own six children.

"My wife keeps a very low profile. She's a homemaker, and a homeschool mom. She doesn't care to be seen. One thing I'm sure about, I would not be CEO of the Durham Rescue Mission without her, period," Tart said.

Lynda smiles when people ask her how much her life changed since Tart became CEO.

"People just thought it would be totally different for me, but it really wasn't. We just keep moving in the same direction. It's not a whole lot different other than having more contact with the volunteers and visiting more churches to present the Mission.

"We like to show how people who have come to the Mission and where they are now—especially people who are on staff who came through the Mission," Lynda said, not knowing her husband had said nearly the same thing.

Tart loves to watch people turn their lives around, and see how God works in their lives. "The stories that I think are the sweetest are not the ones that say thank you, thank you thank you," Tart said. "They are the ones that actually come to work at the Mission."

Their children share their love for the Mission. Their eldest, Katie, who has a degree in accounting, was asked to help the Temps to the Rescue through the years, and still works in Human Resources for the program. Brittany became a nurse at nearby Duke University Hospital. Heidi contributes to the Mission by doing data entry and making thank-you calls to donors. Alexander works in the Training Center, and all the children have supported the Mission through the years in some way.

"I think it's just really special my kids were able to grow up here and see all the people they had the privilege of seeing just come off the streets and grow in the Lord," she said, giving the kids opportunities to help some, even once helping plan and play piano at one couple's wedding.

Until becoming CEO, all through his time at the Mission, Tart volunteered his Sundays to preaching or serving as deacon at various churches and startup congregations in the Raleigh-Durham area, with Lynda always there supporting him. In 2007 they decided they needed a church group of homeschoolers like themselves.

"It doesn't matter whether I am attending church or pastoring a church—a bunch of homeless guys show up," Tart laughed. "Instead of our church becoming a church for homeschoolers, the church became a church for the homeless," he said, and accepts God was trying to tell him something.

Now, he spends his time traveling to different churches as CEO to ask other churches to support the Mission, with Lynda by his side.

Looking back on how it all unfolded, from their original plan to go be foreign missionaries, to their, "roots just growing deeper and deeper," at the Durham Rescue Mission, Lynda thinks it worked out just how it was supposed to.

By 2023, the Mission had five stores, and the income made up about half the annual budget, putting out 250 W-2 tax forms each year while employing an average of 100 clients every week through thrift store operations.

"Money is such a trigger for people with addictions," Tart said. An important part of the Mission's program helps clients learn how to manage money with steady paychecks once they are gainfully employed at the Mission.

Welcome Back. Relapsing a Part of Recovery.

Through the years, Tart said he's seen many people leave multiple times, only to return in the same or worse homeless predicament, needing to restart their recovery.

"I can't think of one that didn't come in and out of here a few times. We don't get upset when they mess up," Tart said. "When the

Client at the Durham Rescue Mission

Early Victory Program class

Lord wants to do His work, He'll do His work. We just have to be ready when He does."

It's the kindness, welcoming spirit, calming and encouraging presence Tart is known for, and one of the reasons people feel supported enough and are willing to return to try again after a setback, instead of letting embarrassment or resentment get in the way.

"You're not seeing people at their best, and they usually do relapse," Tart said. "And come back."

"We recognize it may just be part of the process of them getting where they need to be.

"When the Lord gives up on us, we'll have the liberty to give up on others," Tart said.

~oc~

Undaunted by the Pandemic

~oc~

As the COVID-19 pandemic swept across the globe, figuring out how to protect everyone and keep operating was a challenge for the Mission, where everyone ate and operated in close quarters most of the time.

"In February 2020, when we first started hearing about it, no one knew what to do or how to prepare for it. We just decided, well, we'll do like everything else and deal with symptoms and the people as they come up," Tart said.

Miraculously, the Mission didn't have any COVID cases for months. As other shelters dropped their residency numbers by 50 percent overnight, the Mission filled to capacity.

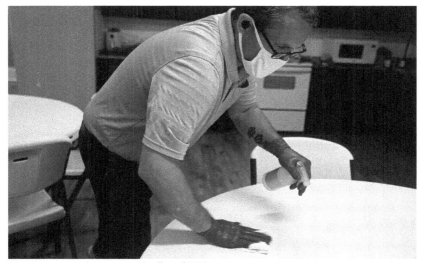

Every precaution was taken to mitigate the effects of COVID.

"Our numbers swelled. We had people everywhere, on the floor. Emergency Management and the Housing Authority people—they were sending more people to us. We were trying to keep new arrivals in the chapel, separated from regular population," Tart said.

The chapel was badly damaged with all the extra use. But the main issue was keeping people separated when they were so crowded.

"When the numbers swelled up like that, we made a decision we've never made before,

We jumped up 350 men, and then more, it was just amazing. We were really over 400 men with nowhere else to go. That's when we made the decision that we're going to stop taking people. We just couldn't keep them separated.

That's when the rumors started that there was COVID at the Mission. No cases were detected or reported. Still, overnight, 150 people left the Mission.

"People were panicking. We had to close our thrift stores because the state required us. At first, they said two weeks, so we carried our people on the payroll for two weeks. We didn't lay anybody off, and we started painting fixing everything we could. We redid some counter tops to make positive use of that time."

But, as COVID raged on, they had to lay off their workers and the thrift store staff.

After several months, the Mission was notified that they could reopen the stores because they were considered essential by providing goods and services.

Ironically, the Mission went months without a single case of COVID. As vaccinations started, and people began going out in the community to receive them, that's when cases began to emerge at the Mission.

Two clients passed away early in the Pandemic. They'd both been vaccinated but had underlying conditions.

As vaccination protections took hold, the Mission reopened the thrift stores. Temps to the Rescue operations got back up to speed in their leased office space at the men's campus.

CHAPTER
Two

From Rescue Mission Campus
to Duke University Campus

Alexander Charles Winn was valedictorian of his 2008 Morehead High School class in Eden, North Carolina. A fair-haired wrestling state champion who scored in the 99th percentile on his SATs, he preferred to be called Alex. His future was bright.

His academic prowess and wrestling power moves drew the attention of Ivy League recruiters. To him, wrestling was like a chess match, played at "a million miles a minute," with moves and countermoves that satisfied his intellect and appeased his natural aggression.

It seemed almost effortless when Winn won a full scholarship to study business and medicine at Duke University. Plus, he landed a spot on the wrestling team.

Maybe it was too easy, he thought, looking back.

Nobody guessed what brewed beneath the surface, the deep feelings of imposter syndrome Winn hid, nor the undiagnosed autism that exacerbated his challenges. They didn't know he used drugs and alcohol to desensitize himself from overwhelming pressures that consumed his mind.

Eden touts its little-town charm and surrounding natural beauty—a garden as it were—a veritable paradise for big outdoor adventure. For Winn, it became the somewhere he needed to escape.

"Small towns have good and bad things. You know everybody, and you have tight-knit support. "But thinking back, I realize that being in a bigger city would have thrown me into a more competitive scene and make me step up my game," said Winn.

He came from a supportive, stable family, he conceded. His mom was a school counselor for behaviorally and emotionally disabled students. With his smarts and successful young life, no one was fully aware of the challenges he faced, not even his mother.

His dad had good jobs, working as a technician for Duke Energy and Proctor & Gamble. He later became a high school and middle school science teacher who served as a youth pastor. He went on church mission trips and cheered on his son's athletic abilities.

Alex Winn and his parents David and Janet Winn

Alex Winn and his parents at graduation from Duke University

Winn was always two steps ahead of any opponent on the wrestling mat.

"I looked at it as I got praised for beating people up. I liked this deal. I always had a lot of aggression, and wrestling was a really nice outlet for that," Winn said.

Eventually, all the moves and countermoves—on and off the mat—got to him. And when the troubles started, he could no longer outmaneuver them.

Wrestling Inner Demons

On the outside, it appeared Winn could do no wrong, but the fresh-faced teen also wrestled powerful inner demons of criticisms, self-doubt and negative patterns. Real or imagined, he felt overwhelmed by pressures to pursue his studies, worship and wrestling. Despite the care and attention his parents poured into him, and perhaps because school seemed easy for him, what he really wanted was to be popular, especially with girls.

"Even girls I thought were really good girls were going for the bad guys," Winn said. "There didn't seem any payoff to being good, but there were lots to being bad. I sought out the people the girls seemed interested in, and tried to be like them."

That meant drinking and smoking marijuana at first, and then he got a girlfriend. "None of it was healthy. That's when I set out to become a drug dealer," he said.

Just like in wrestling, his intellect helped him stay two steps ahead of getting caught. He kept his emotional turmoil, insecurities—and drug activities—under the radar.

Winn had talent. He held his own, reaching the semifinals in his 140-pound weight class in the 2007 Super 32 Wrestling Tournament. The Greensboro, North Carolina-based event drew wrestlers from across the country. Elite scouts watched him defeat the wrestler ranked second in the nation whom they were there to recruit. The assistant coach from prestigious Duke University asked Winn's dad what his son's SAT scores were. They were 1400 and 2200—putting him in the top 1%.

"The truth is, I was high when I took the SAT," Winn said.

False Start: 'Tripping' Through First Semester at Duke

He received the scholarship to Duke and a spot on the wrestling team. Still dealing drugs as he entered college, he didn't make much money. "Rule number one, do not get high on your own dealer supply," he said.

His beer drinking and marijuana use escalated to skipping classes and hiding out in his room for days, getting high on cocaine, LSD, acid or ecstasy—whatever mood-altering chemical was available.

Within one semester, his teenage bravado and careful façade crumbled under the pressures that made him lose his scholarship, faith and self-respect. He was glad when he learned he could quit wrestling, so he could just take classes and party. Then the partying eclipsed the academics. He couldn't pick a major. Even his drug dealing was a "failed endeavor."

"I spent a lot of time just stuck in my room," he recalled. "It chemically affected me. I had unresolved emotional stuff, and anything that would let me change my emotional state, I was into."

He took a medical leave in 2009, more because he didn't want to flunk out than actually get help. He went to rehab, saw a psychologist

Ernie and Gail Mills attended Alex Winn's graduation from Duke University.

Alex Winn receives his Certificate of Completion from Rob Tart and Lynn Holloway at the Durham Rescue Mission's Victory Program graduation.

and returned in the spring of 2010. But he couldn't make it through the full semester. "On some level, I knew I needed help, but I was too sick to know how badly I needed it," he said.

❦

Substance Abuse Stole His Substance for a Decade

❦

After leaving Duke, Winn drifted from job to job, never keeping any for long. There were factories, a wood finishing plant, a T-shirt company, warehouses, and a nameless list of jobs waiting or busing tables at restaurants or doing sales (other than drugs).

"A job was an incidental afterthought so I could keep doing drugs," Winn said.

Later, the drinking picked up. He slept with a bottle of vodka under his pillow and reached for any cocaine, pain pills and amphetamines he could get. He realized he was after the "emotional fix," and had used food and shoplifting the same way before turning to drugs. Before he knew it, nearly 10 years passed since his future seemed so bright.

"My parents let me stay at their house out of sheer love, honestly. I knew how to do just enough to get them off my back. I'd convince them success was just around the corner," he said.

Durham Rescue Mission: From Prodigal to Pathway to Victory Over Addiction

Rock bottom came during a big snow storm in 2018 when he went to get some Gatorade to mix with his vodka. He remembered the car windows fogged up badly because the day before—in a desperate drug-induced frenzy he's embarrassed to say his mom partially videotaped—he tore the paneling out frantically searching for $400 in drug money he lost.

"I'm pulling out of Dollar General, and I remember staring at this cute girl. It must have been more than a quick glance," he said, because when he turned his eyes back to the road, in front of his moving car was, "the sweetest old lady with a walker. I hit my brakes and skid to a stop less than six inches from taking this lady out."

By the time he got home, he was distraught about the near miss and ready for a fight with his prime target, his dad. "I wanted him to raise a finger against me so I could unload a lifetime worth of rage against him," he said.

Instead, he stayed up all night down in his basement bedroom writing all the reasons his parents should pay for him to move to

Durham so he could work his way back into Duke. His mom spent the night at her sister's house to get away from the brewing conflict.

"I realized I was driving a wedge between them and I had to leave. For Dad, it was tough love. So, at this point, I obsessively packed everything."

Winn knew even if he waited for the clothes in the dryer, he'd lose his nerve, so he threw wet things into a bag in the back of his uninsulated car.

He made it to a shelter in Raleigh that night, but didn't like it, so he drove to a nearby IHOP® and slept in his car in the 24-hour restaurant parking lot.

"I got woke up by tap, tap, tap on the window, and it was this nice older couple that said they wanted to buy me a meal. It was the best steak and cheese omelet. I will never forget the kindness of those people," he said.

With nowhere to go, he called his grandmother, Lois Gunter, of Virginia Beach. He knew better than to ask to stay with her, because he'd been so much trouble to her before—but she loved him and did some research about places that provided assistance for drug addicts and alcoholics. She told him about the Durham Rescue Mission.

"She always believed in me. She always prayed for me, had faith in me. She got folks in her Sunday school class to pray for me. She gave me the address, and I went," he said.

The first few weeks at the Mission were during its Operation Rescue Warm Shelter—when the Mission sends out teams to spread the word for anyone sleeping rough in extreme weather conditions to come inside. He slept on the floor of the cafeteria, which suited him just fine.

Winn said no one made him do anything during Warm Shelter, and he'd found a place to park his car so he could hang on to it in case he needed to make a quick getaway. When it came time to check in, living in one of the dorms, he had to follow rules and contribute.

"I was taking clothes off hangers at the Training Center. It was the most tedious, monotonous thing ever," he said.

But he was good at it, and it gave him time to think as he clung harder to his dream of getting back into Duke. Winn thought the Mission had a gift for assigning talent to task and being inclusive of all abilities. He saw others that didn't do well in some jobs thrive in other positions the Mission gave them. For his mathematical mind, sorting things was a good use of his skills.

"Nobody knew I was autistic then, but the intuitive way the Mission worked seemed to end up fairly well. A lot of stimulation, people and sensory stuff really bothered me. But this way, I contributed and helped earn my room and board."

When He Stopped Running His Own Way, God and Friends Walked Alongside

He finally got his turn to apply to the Durham Rescue Mission's Victory Program, which includes biblical classroom training followed by work experience. What surprised him was just how intellectually stimulating he found the sermons after not attending church for years. He even called his dad to tell him. It was deeds not words, though, that softened his heart, as his mentors at the Mission showed him how to apply those familiar messages.

"The doctrine was not new to me, having been raised in the church. It did refresh my knowledge, but really the most important things—and the biggest surprise—was that I learned about taking care of myself, being accountable, being on time, showing up early—having good role models," he said. "I had a lot of intellectual knowledge, but what I needed was the way those men modeled how to live. Just being around people like that was probably the most valuable lesson."

The Victory Program made him realize his Duke dreams couldn't happen with all the drug use, he said. The Mission taught him the life skills and "soft skills" he needed to succeed.

Winn had setbacks at the Mission, and sometimes his thoughts got the better of him. He got moved to a yard crew assignment he didn't like and felt like giving up. But then his grandma called. It was a short conversation. She told him the story of Joseph, and how it wasn't about what life handed to you—but how you responded. That's when scripture started having meaning in his life. "I could memorize this stuff, but couldn't live it before," he said.

Things started falling into place. His grandma encouraged him to contact an administrator at Duke the family knew. He called Duke and learned he might have a chance of getting back in, so he worked up the nerve to call a Duke neuroscience professor.

"I think I came right out with the whole thing and told him everything. I had nothing to lose. I told him I'd completed his free online course and got an A. He was impressed with that, I think, because only a tiny percentage of people finished it. More than anything, though, I think it was my interest in the subject. I really came alive when talking about the human mind and the human brain," Winn said.

The professor told Winn that he ran with some students in Duke Forest, and if he was in the area, he could feel free to join him to talk some more.

"I said I'd love to join you," which may have been a stretch as Winn never liked running in high school. He was so eager and nervous about being on time, he had friends make sure he was up early and ready to catch the bus. On their first run, when the professor asked him what his research interests were, Winn was so winded going up a hill, he had to stop and walk.

"The professor stopped and walked with me," Winn said.

Autism Diagnosis Answers Many Questions

That first run with that neuroscience professor was in May of 2018, and Winn was accepted back into Duke the following spring semester at age 28, 10 years after his first acceptance. Being a Duke student meant he had healthcare, and that's when his reactions to life started

Alex Winn with his Duke University neuroscience professors, Ellen Vos-Wisse and Dr. Leonard White

making sense. He was diagnosed with neurodevelopmental disorders—autism spectrum disorder (ASD) and Attention-Deficit/Hyperactivity Disorder (ADHD).

In Winn's case, his behavior spiraled into self-destructive mood-altering drug abuse, which chemically exacerbated his challenges.

"They thought I had bipolar disorder or social anxiety," he said. "I'm one person when on drugs, another when off.

"The right diagnosis changed everything. So many things in my life made me feel separated. It helped me to find my place in the world. It really did," said Winn, who participates in autism awareness events at Duke.

ⵞⵞ

Out of Brokenness, It All Added Up to God's Math

ⵞⵞ

Not counting the 10 years spent floundering since his disastrous first attempt at Duke, once Winn re-enrolled and was accepted, he found the confidence and support he needed.

When he graduated from the Victory Program and moved into his own place, the first thing he did was go to the Durham Public Library with the letter his grandmother sent him, so he'd have mail at his address. Now he had a library card.

Before he knew it, Winn took the bus from the Durham Rescue Mission's Men's Campus to classes at Duke's historic campus to restart his degree he gave up a decade before.

In only three years, he completed his self-declared major—Mind Science, Neurocognitive Dynamics and Artificial Intelligence – by loading up on summer courses like catching up for lost time.

After graduation, he became a research associate for the math department, working under renown Professor Ingrid Daubechies, the James B. Duke Distinguished Professor of Mathematics and Electrical and Computer Engineering.

A Long Way from Brain Altering Chemicals to Neuroscience Researcher

"A lot of what our brains do is mathematical, and math describes a lot of nature—gravity, magnetism, and recently researchers have been applying it to more information-type systems like computers," Winn said.

Winn excitedly rattled off how his neuroscience major led him to the math department. "Math describes how computers can store and transmit and understand information. My boss is an expert in information theory, which is the magic of how our brains process information," he said.

When asked after he presented a research poster in Washington D.C. in 2023 in front of the Society of Neuroscience if he believed how far he'd come from homelessness in so short a time, Winn's simple answer was, "No. I really can't. It's almost surreal to me.

"I think this whole thing is a God thing. It could not have come together any better. But, it's almost like I didn't have anything to do with it. The change happened—The father doith the works," Winn said, quoting John 14:10.

"I'd never surrendered before—fully surrendered in my life. Being homeless is not fun, and the atmosphere at the Mission was set up to teach you. I think I learned that things work out better when I'm not trying to be in control."

Winn said "a thousand little things" like meals always being on time, and rules with consequences, structure, order, and dress codes helped him move away from his addiction.

"From top to bottom, the whole thing teaches you how to manage. Later on, I became a house manager, where I oversaw the structure there. I saw a whole new level of things, and how it helped people get better. And that gave me confidence," Winn said.

Ultimately, he said, he didn't want to let people down who helped him so much, like Rev. Tart or the director of the Men's Religious Education division, L. Frederick Holloway.

"I knew I could do better, and there were standards, so I worked hard to meet them," he said. All the while he was at the Mission, Winn clung to what he called his "irrational" dream to somehow work his way back into Duke. Though less than six miles apart, for the homeless recovering addict, Duke's iconic ivy-covered Georgian campus at times seemed light years from the Men's Campus at the Mission. That it actually happened was pure grace, he said.

_⸙

Lasting Lessons: 'I Wouldn't Have Any of This Without the Mission.'

_⸙

Even after he graduated from Duke, he said the miracles kept coming. "I found out I only had $10,000 in student loans. That was one of the biggest cries I ever had was leaving the financial aid offices that day," Winn said. "I used to spend every penny I got."

However, at the Mission, Rev. Aaron Gamble, men's chaplain and counselor, taught him to save up. Winn opened a bank account with the money from his stipend.

"Before that, I didn't have a penny to my name," Winn said.

It was a while before Winn felt worthy of all that was restored to his life. Eventually, he began to accept: "I earned this. I belong here. I really did feel that. Through fortitude and resilience. There were times I would wake up really early and I would go into the computer lab at like 6 a.m. and do programming, and I was taking a programming class online at the Mission. Having this really good computer skillsets at the Mission helped me in my life. I learned online through free online classes programming skills that I use to this day.

"I've struggled with imposter syndrome. After the Mission, I'm a totally different person. What a difference a year makes. I'm now living in a house with a friend of mine. I talk on the phone once a week at least to my grandma—and my parents, too. I wouldn't have any of this without the Mission."

"I'm very grateful to the Mission. Why am I tearing up? I honestly look back on that time very fondly."

In 2024, Winn started his PhD at The University of North Carolina at Chapel Hill in the Biological and Biomedical Sciences Program.

He also became engaged to Charlotte Stoute, who he met at Duke in 2010. Stoute studied neuroscience as well, graduating in 2013, and going on to work at the Duke Center for Autism & Brain Development.

"We knew each other briefly 'back in the day,'" Winn said. "But the relationship really never had a chance to develop until I was clean and sober."

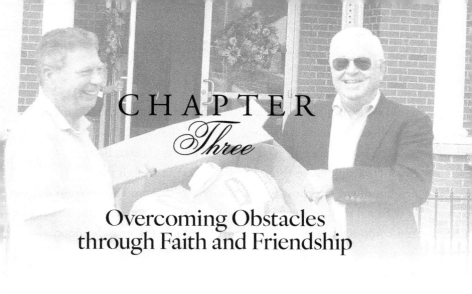

CHAPTER
Three

Overcoming Obstacles through Faith and Friendship

I t's one of those oft-told memorable and dramatic stories about the Mission—how Rev. Ralph E. Clegg helped Gail and Ernie Mills get rid of the cockroaches in the two ramshackle houses where the Mission began. It was like a plague being lifted, illustrating both the faithfulness and significant sacrifices the young couple made to build their dream of serving homeless addicts and their kind-hearted benefactors—without whom the Mission may not have survived.

"When he sprayed, you could hear dead cockroaches hitting the floor. It sounded just like popcorn popping," recalled Gail Mills about the exterminator who helped make the first Mission buildings habitable. "The next day, there were hundreds of dead cockroaches in the bottom of the bathtub."

Ralph Clegg and his son, Philip, who goes by Phil, are steadfast fixtures in Mission history, faithful supporters whose help is woven throughout the Mission's struggles and successes.

In 1974, Ernie and Gail Mills first moved into the two houses in a crime-ridden northeast central Durham neighborhood that began the Durham Rescue Mission. In equal states of disrepair, one building served as a parsonage for their young family. It was previously a rental house but was as neglected as the neighboring abandoned and vandalized house they acquired to serve Mission clients.

The houses were originally owned by the Golden Belt Manufacturing Co. to house their workers. Through the neighborhood's decline, vandalism by vagrants, and decay from decades of deferred maintenance left gaping holes in the uninsulated structures. You could see the ground through the floors. The neighborhood became plagued by drugs, and the houses infested with bugs and rodents.

Ralph Clegg knew the neighborhood well because he lived in Durham and worked nearby for years. He befriended Ernie in those early days. Clegg was also a pastor at a church in Louisburg, a 40-minute drive to Durham, and would invite Ernie to his church to speak, so he could take up a love offering for him.

When Ralph Clegg found out about the infestation, he sent an employee from his pest control business right over to take care of the problem.

Clegg: An Accidental Exterminator

Ralph Clegg didn't start out to work in pest control. His day job was as a machinist for the Golden Belt Manufacturing Co., which was originally founded to produce cotton cloth and thread for smoking-tobacco bags.

Ralph also served as minister at the Saint's Delight Baptist Church in Louisburg, founded in 1885. Having a church in historic Louisburg, home to the nation's oldest private two-year college, Louisburg College,

Clegg couldn't walk down Main Street without passing a picturesque collection of historic churches dotting the oak-lined corridor.

In his youth, Ralph felt called to the ministry, and took correspondence courses through the Moody Bible Institute during the 1950s. Interestingly—and consistent with Ralph's strong heart for homeless missions—the evangelical institute's beginnings took root in 1871 when founder D.L. Moody was ministering to the needs of thousands (one-third of the city) who were left homeless by the "Great Chicago Fire." The institute established the Moody Correspondence School in 1901 for, "the benefit of those of both sexes who cannot, for financial or other reasons, attend the Institute personally."

Ralph ordered as many books as he could. Phil remembers his dad pulling out those Moody Institute books to study and craft his fiery sermons. With his mechanical skills, he even created props to help bring the Bible stories vividly to life.

As much as he "never met a stranger," and was known for his friendly personality, when Rev. Clegg entered the pulpit, you could count on "hellfire and brimstone" fervor in his passionate sermons to rouse the flock, Phil said. He pastored part-time in a couple other churches before settling into a full-time ministry at Saint's Delight.

In 1963, a termite infestation developed in the old Saint's Delight Baptist Church building on Firetower Road. Rev. Clegg asked several termite companies for estimates to control the termites, but they were all too expensive and beyond the small congregation's means.

Through his own determined research and with the help of a friend at North Carolina State University, Ralph learned all he could about termites. He decided he could put his mechanical background and skills to use and build the sprayer equipment himself. Then he convinced one of the local chemical companies to agree to sell him the termite treatment chemicals. Church members pitched in to help him successfully treat the church.

Word spread through the congregation and soon church members were asking Rev. Clegg to treat their homes, too. In 1964, he incorporated Clegg's Termite & Pest Control. Initially, he focused only on termites, but, as his home-based hobby grew into a thriving business, he branched out into other pest control services.

❧

A Family Firm

❧

Ralph continued his work in Durham for Golden Belt Manufacturing and preaching at the Louisburg church.

By 1970, the pest control business was taking off, and he was ready to focus full time on it and his ministry. The problem was, he needed help.

At the time, Phil was working as a forester and pilot with the North Carolina Forest Service in its aerial fire patrol when his dad asked (and his mother pleaded with) him to come help him manage the business. Phil had graduated in 1965 from NC State with a degree in forestry and loved his job.

Still, Phil and wife Brenda, along with their two small girls at the time, packed up a moving van and moved back home to Durham to help Ralph run the family business, and never looked back.

That meant Ralph could retire from Golden Belt, which later closed in 1994. In 2008, the historic brick Golden Belt factory warehouse property was redeveloped as a mixture of residences, artists' studios, office space, and retail.

When he became president of Clegg's, Phil still used his love of flying to visit offices throughout the company's service territory—consistently ranked as one of the largest pest businesses in the country.

In 2023, there were more than 32,000 pest control companies in the U.S. Clegg's ranked 38th largest in Pest Control Technology's annual 100 largest companies listing. With 300 trucks serving three states, Clegg's is usually in the top 50, sometimes in the 30s or even 20s—a far cry from one man using home-made equipment from his house that started it all in 1963.

Phil Clegg's son, Philip Jr., carries on the family business as a company leader, too.

A Legacy of Generosity

Back in 1974, as Ernie was trying to establish the Durham Rescue Mission, Clegg's was well established, and the kindly preacher and business owner Ralph Clegg did what he could to encourage his young protégé.

As Phil Clegg tells it, when the Mission was starting, his dad told him he was hiring a new termite guy.

"I was confused because we didn't need a termite guy," Phil Clegg said.

Ralph retorted, brooking no discussion: "Well, Ernie Mills needs a job to feed his family. We're hiring him as a termite guy," Phil chuckles, recalling the memory and his dad's determination to help.

"My dad was just that kind of guy. He'd give you the shirt off his back if you needed it," Phil said.

As for why the son continues to support the Mission, his reply is simple: "The Lord has been good to our business. We've done very well, and I figured I'd contribute some of that back."

Back in 1974, Ernie soon got busy with speaking engagements and running the Mission. His tenure as a pest control technician was short-lived, lasting less than a year. His friendship with the Clegg family – father and son – endured.

Ralph, who retired but remained active in the business for years afterward, died in 1999.

Phil recalls Ernie and Gail coming to visit him on Sept. 11, 2001. He remembers his secretary frantically running in and out of the meeting reporting that the Twin Towers had been hit by terrorists, and then the Pentagon. Undeterred, Ernie and Gail were there to discuss the new building they planned to build next to the church building they'd acquired to expand the Mission in 1978—the place where they'd moved from those original houses Ralph Clegg helped them with. The Mission outgrew even its new quarters, and because of their long-standing support, they wondered if Clegg would want to help sponsor it and have the family name on one of the rooms.

"Ernie, I can't afford to pay for it. So, Ernie said, 'That's fine. You can have five years.' Ernie's very clever like that," Phil Clegg smiles. The deep friendship continued through the years.

In 2013, the 250-seat dining room at the Mission's Center for Hope was named in honor of Ralph and his wife, Mildred Clegg. The Center for Hope, next to the East Main Street Durham Rescue Mission church, has a commercial kitchen, classroom space for the Victory Program, a GED classroom, computer lab, and three dormitories for the Men's division, and represented a growth beyond what Ernie ever envisioned.

It was not done growing. Ernie and Gail came and wanted Clegg to sponsor another dormitory building. Once again, Clegg once again told Ernie he couldn't pay for it. And once again, Ernie nodded amiably and told him that was fine, he could take five years.

When Phil brought the proposal to Brenda to ask what she thought, she answered by turning the question around to ask Phil what he thought his father, Ralph, would want. That was the end of the discussion. A Clegg dormitory it would be.

Clegg sponsored the construction of the new Clegg Family Student Housing, which opened in 2019 with 54 beds, kitchen, dining room, and TV room.

In another one of those full-circle moments, at the building dedication, the Mission asked one of its clients to speak about their experience and what the generosity of building the dorm would mean to his life. That client was John Davis. After he spoke, Davis sought out Phil Clegg to thank him for sponsoring the dorm, but also to tell him about a connection he had to the company.

"My grandmother used to work for you," Davis told Clegg.

"Who was your grandmother?" Clegg asked.

It turned out Davis' grandmother worked for Clegg for 30 years and retired from the company.

"I couldn't believe it. I told him if he had any kind of work ethic like your grandmother, you gotta come to work for me," Clegg said.

Clegg asked Ernie if John could be assigned to Clegg's for his work rotation through the Victory Program and rekindled his friendship with Davis' grandmother.

Clegg knew the troubles Davis' family endured because his mother fell into drug addiction. Clegg understood how Davis wound up needing the Mission to help him.

He gave Davis his first job after the Mission. "He was a very good loyal employee. He'd catch the bus here, and we got so we'd send folks to pick him up." Davis went on to a successful career in heating and air conditioning, along with starting his own ministry, and continues to be involved with the Mission.

Showing that same compassionate understanding and lack of judgement that inspired his dad to do all he could to help the Mission help redeem and rebuild lives, Phil Clegg said: "I knew what his grandmother had gone through. As a teenager and young adult, John was born in that environment. He got off on the wrong foot with the wrong crowd."

CHAPTER
Four

From Big and Bad to 'Big Blessed John'

John Davis could always hold his own in a fight. Good thing, too, because otherwise, Friday night fights in state prison would have been really rough for him.

He was always ready for a fight. He'd hung out with rough crowds since he was 13 and started dealing drugs at 15.

At 19, Davis landed in the former Polk Youth Institution, a processing center for male offenders ages 19–21 in Butner, North Carolina. After being held on $350,000 bond, he was sentenced to 27 months on 16 counts of felony drug trafficking and distribution of narcotics.

"Every Friday night, the inmates would have fights. They would pick bunk numbers, and you'd have to fight the other one that was picked. Pretty much you would have to fight for your life, ensuring your stability while you were in prison," said Davis.

"I never had any issues. I could fight. Still, it's something that affects you emotionally for the long-term," he said, adding it should have been a turning point for him to find a better path.

It wasn't.

Before he wound up in state prison, nobody would have expected Davis—with his keen intellect and athletic potential—was headed there. Here was a gifted student who scored 1350 on his SAT and received academic and sports scholarships. To say the least, state prison was a surprising outcome for the promising young man who graduated in the top 10 of his class of 250 students at Orange High School in his hometown of Hillsborough, North Carolina.

Hillsborough, a quintessential small town that celebrates a big history, is the county seat of Orange County in central North Carolina. A popular haven for artists and writers, Hillsborough is full of charm and character with lots of notable old homes, and is listed on the National Register of Historic Places. With a thriving downtown life, it is surrounded by abundant natural beauty and attractions like the Occoneechee Mountain State Natural Area and Riverwalk, a greenway along the Eno River, which is part of the N.C. Mountains-to-Sea Trail.

Davis was raised by his dad in these picturesque outward surroundings. That wholesome environment could not safeguard him from the unhealthy inner turmoil and feelings of abandonment he suppressed from a young age.

Broken Family, Broken Hearted Boy

His parents divorced when Davis was six. He didn't see his mother because of her drug use after that.

"She moved away and I'd go see her every now and again, but Dad forbade it unless it was with my grandma because she was still using drugs," Davis said.

"My dad grew up like that. I later learned my grandpa was a part of the Hell's Angels. My dad never did drugs, but at some point, he'd been involved in selling them. He'd gotten out of that life, and he wanted to protect me from it," Davis said.

All Davis knew as a child was that his mother was absent. And it shattered his wellbeing.

"A lot of people said I didn't show it on the outside—that I was sad. But I held resentment in my heart for a long time," said Davis. Still, he considers his upbringing "privileged."

"I didn't have a motherly figure, but my dad was a great father. He provided and taught me to work hard for what I had, and that nothing was going to be given to me," said Davis.

Davis played football, baseball and basketball starting at the age of five. Sports became an outlet and stand-in for his unexpressed anger and aggression—a substitute for the hurt he felt. It was a way to cope with the loss of his mom's presence in his life.

John Davis and daughter, Jubileigh

"Success just came too easy to me. I overcompensated in my life," he said.

His downhill slide started at about 13 when he attended a high school party and his first taste of alcohol, another way to numb he pain. One cup of beer turned into "copious amounts of alcohol," and led to marijuana. He called it the "smell of a good time," that became his addiction.

"I had a business-inclined mind, and I knew so many people who wanted to buy marijuana, so I figured why not do what I want for free. I began to deal heavily by age 15 or 16, selling large amounts of marijuana. I'd make $5,000 to $10,000 a week in high school," Davis said.

∾

College Didn't Fit His 'High' Lifestyle

∾

He started attending college, but soon just couldn't see the profit in all the hard work and discipline.

"The lifestyle didn't match up with the life I was living. Why would I do this if I'm making more than the teachers?" He dropped out quickly and before he knew it, at age 19, landed in state prison for more than a year.

"You come out of prison and you say, 'I'll do it differently. I'll be able to change,'" he said. Perhaps predicably, within six months he was hanging out with the same people, doing exactly what he used to do and headed for trouble.

"I was a felon trying to get a job. I was resilient, though. I pushed forward, and I didn't see anything wrong with it," Davis said. He

John Davis and wife, Jenifer

drove nice cars, wore expensive clothes, and carried backpacks full of $40,000 in cash.

"I didn't see myself as a drug addict, because it didn't affect my income. I was not on the corner begging for money. It was a self-righteousness that I was somehow better. But I had the exact same problems they had."

All the money and what he could buy with it—"That was my happiness, where I found contentment," he said. "It was greed. If I had five, I wanted 10. But I could never fill the loneliness and void that I had."

His life became a roller coaster of riding high, making "easy" drug money followed by lows of getting arrested, sitting in county jail awaiting his next trial. His addiction grew and expanded into opiates, becoming a revolving door cycle he couldn't escape.

"The last detention center I was in; I was on 24-hour lockdown. There were no books, other than the Bible," he said.

His grandparents were a big influence in his young life before drugs took over. They instilled in him that he should go to church on Sunday morning and evening, and Wednesday nights, too. He remembered wanting to grow up to be like his grandfather.

It's not like he'd never heard the gospel his grandparents wanted him to know. It's just that he only got exposed to it occasionally, maybe at Easter or Christmas, and he was too young, distracted, or overwhelmed during those infrequent hectic holiday extravaganzas for it to make an impact on him.

Awaiting trial with nothing better to do while sitting in lockup, he opened that Bible. He started with the books of John and Matthew. To underscore his mindset at the time, Davis paused to observe that chose those two solely for the self-centered reason that they are his first and middle names.

"Matthew began to speak of the birth of Christ. Then I went to read John, and that hit me differently," he said, explaining he suddenly realized he blamed everyone else for his problems instead of taking responsibility for his own actions.

"Everything in my life that happened to me was my fault," he said, remembering how the Bible verses struck him in his holding cell. "It was not my mom's fault for not being there. Not my dad for not bailing me out. Not my friends for not helping me."

Trials and Then His Own Conviction

Davis wasn't sure how to find his way out, so, he tried bargaining with God.

"I prayed a prayer that was really, really selfish. I prayed that, 'Lord, if you get me out of this predicament this one time, I'll serve you.' But God knew my heart at that moment. He knew I was ready for a change. And I knew there was more to life than the life I was living," Davis said.

He began to realize he'd been trying to fill a void in his life with money and power, but he never felt truly fulfilled or happy. He never felt peace.

It was 2018, and he also realized his life of crime caught up with him. He knew with multiple past convictions; he couldn't avoid incarceration because of mandatory sentencing guidelines. At that point, he was a four-time convicted felon, which meant mandatory prison. Or so he thought.

God, it seems, had other plans.

Davis recalled that day of brokenness as he faced what he expected to be his inevitable sentencing.

"I remember my dad was on the stand that day testifying against me. He was saying he couldn't give me the help I needed. I'd never seen my dad cry in my life, and tears were running down his face."

To everyone's surprise, the judge placed Davis on 15-months of probation with the condition that he must attend a year-long rehabilitative program. Davis chose the Durham Rescue Mission, a place he'd heard about from a case worker when he was facing other drug charges in the Orange County Jail.

"I'd been in jail for 10 months, and I walked straight to Bojangles and got me some food. Then I walked straight to Grandma's. She was my motherly figure—my mom's mom. She'd do anything for me, but that day she wouldn't even come to the door. I could hear her talking through the door to me," Davis said.

Davis knew it was hard for her to do that. She'd always tried to fill the void his mother's drug addiction had left in his life.

"The truth is, she probably thought if she let me in, I wouldn't make it to the Durham Rescue Mission that day. My dad was the same. He wouldn't let me in, but he gave me $40 and some of my clothes. I understand why," Davis said.

July 9, 2018

That was July 9, 2018, and Davis did make it to the Mission. It was so crowded, he slept on the floor of the main cafeteria at first.

"They assign you work duty and I've done construction, so I said I'll go help in maintenance," Davis said. "I met my supervisor, Joel Dedic. He was a very nice man; a very good Christian man who would be nice to you and do whatever he could for you."

> " The Mission changed my life and the future of my children's lives and made it so we're able to live the life God wanted us to. I will always be so thankful for the burden that Mr. Ernie Mills had. "
>
> John Davis

Davis said each morning while riding to their assignments at different buildings, Dedic would witness to him, expanding on a passage of scripture and sharing how Jesus wanted to save him.

"We were going to Home Depot, and I said, 'Man, we were going the longest way possible. I know how to get to Home Depot from here,'" Davis said with a laugh, knowing that Dedic deliberately went out of his way so he could talk longer and help him.

All the while, Dedic shared the gospel, and on their long drives to Home Depot, he'd ask Davis if he was 100% sure if he died, he'd go to heaven. "He would let it go when he knew it was too much for me to take, but he never gave up on me."

"One day, I said I was 75%. I had so much guilt and blame for all the bad that I had done in my life, and the chaos I'd started in other individual's lives. I've seen people strung out on drugs I sold, and they had kids, or they were somebody's child or mother or father. It wasn't just that person I was doing harm to. I didn't think God could forgive me for that," Davis said.

Dedic told Davis God would forgive all things.

July 21, 2018: 'Since then, it's wild thinking about what God has done.'

Just 12 days after he'd arrived at the Mission, Davis said while he could hardly believe God could forgive his misdeeds, when Dedic explained that he could and would, he grasped at it.

"That was like, man, I need that right now. So, under the contractor bay of the Home Depot parking lot, I accepted the Lord as my savior. It was July 21, 2018, and it was like a weight was lifted off my shoulders immediately. Since then, it's just wild thinking about what God has done."

Davis entered the Victory Program, graduating in August 2019. He joyfully recounts the many blessings that haven't stopped since, he said.

After Victory Program, he was assigned to live in a newly constructed dorm at the Mission called the Clegg Family Center, built as a transitional step for clients to leave the Mission. At such dedication ceremonies for new building, the Mission likes to have a client give their testimony. Since Davis would be living in the new facility, they asked him to share what changes he experienced since he came to the Mission.

As he spoke, he realized he had a connection to the donors who funded his new residence hall. After the ceremony, Davis told Gail Mills that his grandmother—Frances Stevens—his mom's mom, that motherly figure growing up whose heart he knew he'd broken more

John Davis and daughter, Jubileigh

John's daughter, Jubileigh, and son, Judah

than once—retired from Clegg's Termite and Pest Control, the Clegg family business.

Unbeknownst to the Mission staff when they asked him to speak, his grandma worked for the company founder for many years as his secretary. Now he'd be living in a residence named after her old boss's company, Clegg's Termite and Pest Control, which was also a long-time supporter of the Mission.

Not only would their generosity house Davis, Clegg's gave him his first job after graduating from the Victory Program.

"These are connections only God can make," said Gail Mills.

More Blessings

Later, in October 2019, a woman messaged Davis on Facebook after reading his testimony shared on the Mission's website. She was studying youth ministry and business at Crown Bible College in Tennessee.

"We began to talk, and I ended up asking her father if I could court her and get to know her better," Davis said.

In October 2021, Davis married that woman, Jenifer, "Jeni." He gleefully tells the story of how he prayed her family "slap into North Carolina," because of a series of events that brought the family from another state for a job opportunity for Jenifer's mom.

Earlier in 2021, Davis moved on from the job with Clegg's to a heating, ventilation and air conditioning company. He was finally putting to good use his Associate of Applied Science degree in Air Condition, Heating, and Refrigeration Technology from Alamance Community College he'd managed to complete after high school. He didn't expect such a great job opportunity with his criminal record.

That year, Davis also finished an associate's degree in theology from Cedar Grove Baptist Bible College, a Mebane, North Carolina-based satellite of Macedonia Baptist College in Midland, North Carolina.

More Blessings Than He Could Count

Then, he and Jenifer welcomed their first child, Jubileigh Marie, in July 2022. Their son, Judah, was born in March 2024.

He can hardly contain the joy or count all the blessings in his life, and he described each one as a miracle that never should have happened to him. He told the story of how his family bought their first house with awe.

"I knew the Lord was going to throw it in my way just when I needed it. I was taking a guy home from work, and there was a really nice trailer for rent, and I said, 'Hey, take a picture of that and send it to my wife,'" Davis said.

When he called, the landlords said they'd been praying for Christian tenants, and they even knew Davis' family. Of course, they knew of the Durham Rescue Mission. He and Jenifer moved into the trailer, and about six months later, the landlords approached them with an unexpected offer about a rental property they wanted to give them the opportunity to purchase. All they had to do was make the down payment.

Happy homeowners John and Jeni

John and Jubileigh praying

"Especially in this market, it was exactly what we prayed for in a house. There were little details that showed God knew our heart. In the last three-and-a-half years, God has reconciled my relationship with Him and, most importantly, He's reconciled my life and my family. He's blessed me, and has given me a wife that wants to serve the Lord with me," he said.

Before the couple married, they traveled around North Carolina each Sunday, sharing their message at various churches about, "the fruitfulness of their giving" to the Mission.

Davis wrote gospel tracts for prison ministries with his testimony of what the Mission did in his life and heart, which the Mission gives to men as they check in.

Full Circle: Reconciliation and Restoration

Davis also reconciled with his mother.

"I had to forgive her. I had to realize I was under that same influence of drugs. I came to the realization that I was just like that. It's not her. It's the drugs that held her. She's going with me to church on Mother's Day," Davis said in 2022.

The following year, he said: "I was able to lead her to the Lord, discipling her, and our relationship is restored. She's doing well."

He also remains close to his father and grandparents and is amazed at all God mended in his life.

As he settled into family life, he and Jenifer started a volunteer children's ministry at their home church, Wayside Baptist Church

John and Jenifer dedicating their daughter, Jubileigh, with the Mills and Pastor Brad Williams and wife, Michelle

in Hillsborough. Every Sunday, they take three church vans into underprivileged neighborhoods to pick up children for Sunday school.

"It's something that was on my heart. I grew up maybe a mile from that church, and I'd never heard the gospel before. A lot of kids miss those opportunities to trust Christ and avoid decisions they'll regret, like the ones I made because I didn't understand it," he said.

The blessings kept coming. In fact, his pastor likes to call him "Big Blessed John," Davis said with a laugh.

Still in his HVAC job, by 2023, he was promoted to field service supervisor, something he marveled at with his background. With Jenifer's help, he began writing a book about his experiences to share his testimony. He hopes, "It can affect the person that's in that situation, and it can help a family member to not give up."

Davis continues to serve at the Mission every Friday night, teaching in the addiction recovery program, sharing the gospel and leading men to Christ weekly.

"It's a blessing to be able to go back to where I was saved," he said.

"The Mission changed my life and the future of my children's lives and made it so we're able to live the life God wanted us to. I will always be so thankful for the burden that Mr. Ernie Mills had."

CHAPTER
Five

From Home Runs
to Homelessness to Hope

G rowing up in St. Pauls, North Carolina, Adam Todd describes his early life as pretty much all a kid could wish for.

St. Pauls in Robeson County calls itself "The Little Town With The Big Heart," harkening back to a kind Mayberry-esque Americana that makes you nostalgic. The community still gathers for a lot of events in the town center. It touts its working-class history of cotton mills and textile trade that flourished when the Virginia and Carolina Railway came through in the early 20th century. St. Pauls is a patriotic place, with roots, about 18 miles southwest of Fayetteville, which is home to Fort Liberty (formerly Fort Bragg), the world's largest military base, and the storied 82nd Airborne Division.

Todd describes himself as that typical lucky, happy kid, with good grades who was good at sports. His Vietnam War veteran dad, his hero, cheered him on at every baseball game—because he was his coach, along with being his biggest fan.

"We were always very close," Todd said.

"Our family—my little brother, Jacob, and I—never wanted for anything. My dad was a police officer. My mom did online marketing (for the Fayetteville Observer newspaper) and I kind of grew up in your prototypical American home," Todd said of his almost idyllic, stable, traditional childhood family life.

Simply put, life was great—until his dad's lung cancer diagnosis.

The asbestos his dad was exposed to in the war took him within six months of the diagnosis. Todd was 14 and about to start high school.

After his father's death, he, his mother and brother moved in with his grandmother, "Mawmaw," who lived in Fayetteville.

He played varsity baseball all four years of high school. He even had offers to go play for colleges when he graduated. Instead, he joined the Army and shipped out to Port Sill, Oklahoma.

But that didn't work out too well, and he ended up with a medical discharge. When he got back, he decided maybe college seemed like a good idea after all.

That didn't work out too well, either. His Mawmaw got sick and died in 2013, leaving the family without the financial resources to pay his tuition.

Adam and Elisabeth Todd's wedding day with Rob Tart officiating

Adam Todd at a the Durham Rescue Mission's Thanksgiving event

He dropped out of college, and started working full time. He was holding his own, doing okay.

But then came another blow. His mother died of congestive heart failure December 29, 2016.

"I went into a spiral of self-pity. I didn't think of my brother at all, who was only 14," he remembered of that dark time.

His little brother Jacob moved in with their uncle, and Adam fell in with the wrong crowd.

"I started smoking marijuana, and progressed to prescription pain killers. It took everything from me. I had no job, no place to live, no vehicle. I started couch surfing, drifting from friend's house to friend's house.

"I remember sitting at my friend's house, and I saw on Facebook, friends were graduating from college, or another one was getting married, and here I was wasting my life away,"

That's when he checked himself into a detox facility in Lumberton, North Carolina, about 35 miles from Fayetteville. At that facility, he met someone who had overcome his addiction and explained the only way he could do it it was salvation through the Lord Jesus Christ.

"I'd tried everything. I said I'm willing to try. He told me about the Durham Rescue Mission," Todd said.

He hopped on a megabus from Fayetteville to Durham, and checked into the Mission. That was June 14, 2019.

"I was overwhelmed with how many people were here to support me," Todd said. "I was sitting in chapel, and they had a guest preacher. I felt like every point he made he was poking me right in the middle of my chest. I felt conviction, but my pride took hold and I wasn't going up there."

As the altar call continued without him, he opened the Bible in his hands, which fell open to Psalm 143:11 and read, "Quicken me, O LORD, for thy name's sake..."

Adam and Elisabeth at the 2021 Annual Fall Banquet

"I went right up to the altar and gave my life to the Lord," he said.

Todd enrolled in the Mission's Victory Program. The first six months of the program is classroom-based biblical training. Then the Temps to the Rescue agency offered him a job picking up donations for the Mission's thrift stores.

After graduating from the year-long Victory Program, the Mission offered him a staff position as their annual fund specialist, which was only the beginning of the opportunities he said unfolded for him.

"It reminds me of the first night I came to the Mission. They're always there for you. I got in really late. I remember the guy who met me was going over everything, and he said, 'You're going to be doing a whole lot, but don't worry. Just sit still.'"

"It's amazing how much God kept blessing me as I was just sitting still," Todd said.

"I went to a conference, and met a lady, who came to work for the Mission. We started dating," Todd said. He married Elisabeth Perkins, executive administrative assistant to Mission CEO Rob Tart, in May of 2022.

"At first, we weren't sure where we were going to live, so we ended up staying in an apartment with the Mission. But then we were able to purchase a home in October of 2022," an event he says still amazes him.

The next January, 2023, he was promoted to Director of Development, another awe-inspiring moment in his journey.

"When they hired me on as their annual fund specialist, my main focus was direct mail and digital marketing program—coming in with zero direct mail and zero marketing experience," his mother's experience notwithstanding.

"But I was trained by the guy who did the job before for 15 years or so, Tony Gooch. He took me under his wing. Here at the Mission, when you get one thing down, it's amazing what else you can get done," he laughed.

He moved on to coordinating fundraising banquets, golf tournaments, and clay shoots for the Mission, and then moved on to learning about managing social media, because some people were transitioning due to retirement and job changes.

One day when he was dropping something off at the Mission, and Rob Tart asked if he could see him in his office.

"At first, I started thinking what did I do…ha. Then he said he wanted me to manage the website and promote me to director of development. It's very intimidating. I took the job so serious, because to think about how I was able to come to the Mission, I didn't have to pay for anything. I'm paving the way for the next person. My work, the labor that I get to put in, is having a direct impact on the next client at the Mission," he said.

"I look back, and so much has changed in a five-year period, and to think all the things God has done. If you think of all the things you did wrong, all the stumbling points. To think He showered me with mercy beyond my comprehending…

Todd's story trailed off as he recalled how he lost contact with his younger brother Jacob when he was living couch to couch and doing drugs. "My uncle kept me away, because he was protecting my brother," he said.

But, once he came to the Durham Rescue Mission, he began going back to Fayetteville to visit Jacob.

"By Jacob seeing the complete 180 degree turn in my life, he went back to church, and got saved. He's in the Army working on helicopters. God has completely restored our relationship together," Todd said.

CHAPTER
Six

A Training Center for How to Live

◠◡◠

Overcoming Fears, Finding Purpose and Dignity

◡◠◡

Kyle Drewry doesn't make excuses. He refers to his youth with only a hint of irony as "your standard American childhood," where his father was addicted to crack cocaine during Kyle's teenage years and his mother later died of an opioid overdose.

Unfortunately, he acknowledges, the lifestyle isn't really that uncommon. Added to the toxic mix, Drewry's family relationships were also strained due to intrigue and disputes over who should get an anticipated inheritance from his wealthy grandparents.

"Life was stressed," said Drewry. "It was a colorful upbringing."

Drewry, his sister, mom and dad lived in a manufactured home owned by his grandparents in the rural Harnett County town of Angier, North Carolina. He spent his youth ruled by feeling unloved, "useless," and as a virtual shut-in, as he put it. He was distrustful and wary of others, left to his own devices, spending his hours alone on the computer, lost in video games. He was good at the games, but by shutting out human interaction, he was ill-equipped for how to interact in society.

He managed to complete high school, after which his father left the family. Drewry then drifted from job to job, lacking the social and "soft" skills needed to succeed.

At 24, Drewry's grandparents called to ask him to come home and care for his mother, whose health had declined mainly due to obesity-related health problems and her reliance on prescription pain medicines.

"I came home, but it wasn't good. My mother needed my help, and having me there stopped her from being lonely, but it was a bad situation. The neighbors all knew my mother had those drugs, and they did not think I was their friend," Drewry said.

It's not that his mother sold the opioids, but neighborhood teens would beg her for them, and she didn't always know how to say no if she thought they were in pain.

"Things came to a head at my mother's house. I called my grandparents and demanded they come down and see what I had seen and help me because I felt like I was going crazy," Drewry said.

"I told them, 'We're all leaving this trailer park, I demand it.' For better or worse, I got my wish. They sold the house out from under my mother," and his mother was sent to a rehabilitation center, he said. With his mother's care needs sorted, Drewry found a job as a Subway store manager.

"I couldn't hold the job. I had social issues and some physical issues," including a congenital leg issue, which had only gotten worse through atrophy from too much video game play and not enough exercise.

"I was ill-prepared for life, to take the next step to be successful. I failed and lost my job. I wasn't fired. I quit, because I knew I couldn't do it. I knew I was going to be homeless. All my life I'd worried about becoming homeless," Drewry said, almost like a self-fulfilling prophecy.

So, he took a practical approach. He got a tent, a small grill and some hot dogs to get him through the weekend, with plans to go to the nearby Raleigh Rescue Mission the following Monday.

"They checked me in, and I was there for a year. I succeeded there, but I did not improve, nor put focus on the things I needed to. I still blamed everyone else," Drewry said of his continued struggle with emotional issues from childhood trauma.

When he left the Raleigh Rescue Mission, he had a job and was living in a hotel with a roommate. "That didn't last, of course," he said, as the downward cycle began again.

"I heard about the Durham Rescue Mission and decided to come here. It was a little bit of shame, and I also knew there was limited space back at the Raleigh Rescue Mission," Drewry said.

Generational Trauma and Escaping a 'Root of Bitterness'

Drewry checked into the Durham Rescue Mission in 2015. He said he recognized he needed help, and took responsibility for what had happened, instead of blaming others.

"At this point, I told myself I'm going to listen and do the things they say," Drewry said. "I had been so bitter. If I thought anybody was slighting me, I could not let it go one bit, to the point where it was detrimental. I couldn't sleep. It was generational."

Drewry said he began to change the blame game to understand that while he "wasn't raised right," and blame his grandparents for not raising his mother right, he realized they probably didn't have much of a foundation, either.

"Mom had her own lifestyle of broken dreams and broken promises," Drewry said.

About five months into the Victory Program, while sitting in Wayside Baptist Church in nearby Hillsborough, North Carolina, Drewry said a little girl was singing about how the Lord had provided the food on her table and shoes on her feet. The words struck a chord and the messages he'd began to understand in his head began to reach his heart.

Drewry learned about the root of bitterness (Hebrews 12:14–15) in the Victory Program, he said. It's when the heart harbors hostility, which grows deeper when someone doesn't deal with hurt by the grace of God.

Listening to the little girl sing, he realized everything he had—from a bed, to clothing, to meals, to the shoes on his feet—had been given to him. "And I didn't deserve it," he said.

"I started crying," Drewry said. "I went down there and got saved on Christmas Eve the week after I got here, but I think that was me submitting. I knew I couldn't do it on my own. I was sincere, but that moment in church, when that little girl started singing, in that moment, I knew."

After completing the requirements of the Victory Program, Drewry decided to check out of the Durham Rescue Mission the day before he was supposed to graduate from the Victory Program.

"It happens a lot. You've been here so long, every little thing upsets you, and you want to be on your own. I thought I was just going to deliver pizzas, play video games, and live with some random person. I knew it was a big mistake that night," Drewry said.

He was back at the Mission within a couple of months.

This time, he made a commitment to himself, "I'm going to go all the way and do all the things they want me to do."

<hr/>

Success, and Then Another Lesson

"This time, I went back to work at the same store. I was determined to be such a valuable member of the team they'd have to hire me. I became a cashier, and was trying to work my way up," Drewry said.

He also started Bible college, and things were going well. So well, in fact, he was promoted to store manager.

"That was a hard transition," Drewry said, once again finding he was ill-prepared when he actually "got what he wanted."

Kyle Drewry working the cash register at the Durham Rescue Mission Thrift Store in Wake Forest, NC

Durham Rescue Mission Thrift Store on Chapel Hill Boulevard in Durham, NC

The challenge for Drewry was feeling like everyone immediately stopped being his friend once he wasn't their peer at work. The competition got to him, and the stress brought back those dreaded sleepless nights. He asked to be demoted.

He gladly went back to being a cashier at another store, but soon was asked to help open another store in another town.

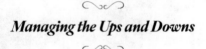

Managing the Ups and Downs

Drewry became the manager to get the store open but told his co-worker once the store was up and running, he'd support him being manager, because he wanted to avoid a repeat of his first attempt at manager.

After a year, Drewry found himself once again being promoted to manager, but this time he "had an absolute blast." The store was running great and Drewry had none of his previous issues.

That is, until 2021 when he mistakenly called the police about a woman he thought walked out of the store without paying for some items.

"She was not happy, because she did buy it. She just didn't have a bag. I'm glad that happened. I learned a lot that day," Drewry said.

He got demoted, but was happy to still have a job as an assistant manager. By that time, he'd moved into an apartment, and his grandparents were glad of his progress, even helping him with a down payment for a car.

Competitive Crossroads Leads to Building on Strengths

Things went well for him back at his previous store as assistant manager. That is, until a disagreement with his district manager, which brought back all the competitive challenges he faced before, made him decide to quit unless he got moved. Drewry ended up at the Mission Training Center as an assistant warehouse manager, a position that needed to be filled quickly, and he fit the need.

"I feel it was serendipity, divine providence. It feels pretty destined," Drewry said.

"I loved the transition. I'm very logistically minded. I love making things more efficient so it's easier for everyone. I'm head of the clothing apparatus," where donations get sorted and priced for distribution to the Mission Thrift Stores.

"We're trying to make it into more real-world transferrable skills. Like we just led a forklift safety class," Drewry said.

Drewry said the Training Center also added classes in soft skills, such as conflict resolution.

"People here need to know how to deal with anger. They need to know how to deal with a supervisor who has an attitude. I didn't know how to deal with it. I would just quit. At least here, I got the support I needed. And now I know I can take classes, too, to overcome my isolationism," Drewry said.

Drewry relishes aiding those whom society rejects and helping them be successful and learn new skills.

"I tell the store managers, 'Send me the worst you got.' These are people that can't make it to the stores. Some may have low IQ or learning disabilities, issues from drug addiction," he said.

"Here, we can tailor a job instead of making the person change to fit the program. We've got to be able to fit in the people that don't fit in anywhere," Drewry said.

ᢙᡃᢚ

Literally and Figuratively Learning to Stand on His Own Two Feet

ᢙᡃᢚ

Looking back on his childhood, Drewry reflects on his self-consciousness and fear of going out in public. Part of it had to do with his leg problem. He'd spent so much of his life sitting and playing video games, he literally couldn't stand for eight hours a day.

"I was pretty depressed about that, too. But here, I couldn't just sit and have a pity party. I had to go to work, even if I was hurt or depressed. I had to face my fears. My manager gave me the breaks

I needed. And eventually, I could stand on my own two feet for the whole day," Drewry said. "Structure is the cornerstone that I needed. I needed somebody to tell me I couldn't lay in bed no more. This place helps you face those fears."

The Mission also provided examples, and Drewry said he watched how his mentors walked and talked and held themselves. He also was focused on mostly their selfless way of helping other people.

"I'm just so grateful for what we do here, and to be a part of it," he said. Working through his issues took physical, spiritual and emotional effort, he said.

"Growing up, it was in the forefront of my mind that people were judging me. Now, I'm more secure in who I am and what I'm doing," Drewry said. "I have dignity."

CHAPTER
Seven

A Voyage to Forgiveness through Troubled Waters

<hr>

"I Forgave You. You Can Forgive Yourself."

<hr>

S helia (pronounced She-la) Joyce spent 22 years in the United States Coast Guard, often supporting the rescue of people in maritime distress. Drowning in her own sea of depression and years of alcoholism, the one person she couldn't "rescue" or forgive was herself—until she found her way to the Durham Rescue Mission.

Looking back on those years in the service, she recalled finding it odd that refugees would flee countries like Haiti, carrying only what they could fit into pillowcases. Invariably, their Bibles were among their meager "necessities." Now she sees that quite differently.

It took spending time at the Durham Rescue Mission to learn why.

Today, buoyed by her newfound—or rather renewed—faith, finding ways to share that lifeline with others is now a lifelong passion.

But her journey took a while.

She was grateful to finally understand God forgave her for wasting so many years in her addiction.

As she stole away for a quiet moment of contemplation on a bench in the gazebo of the garden at the Durham Rescue Mission's Good Samaritan Inn—she just had one problem.

She said it out loud as she prayed.

"I can't forgive myself," she told God.

Instantly, she was taken aback when God answered right back to her heart.

"Do you think you're better than me?"
"What! No, of course I'm not better than you!" she replied.
"I forgave you. You can forgive yourself."

"I think the Lord puts thoughts in your head," she said.

Pollard-Lindsey Garden at the Good Samaritan Inn

Shelia Joyce serving in the United States Coast Guard

It was a life-changing realization that helped her successfully stay sober, when she couldn't so many times before when she tried on her own.

She grew up in Mebane, in Orange County, North Carolina, a city which straddles the Research Triangle and the Piedmont Triad regions. Her family was Baptist, so they were in church every Wednesday night and twice on Sunday. She accepted Christ at age nine, much to the delight of her faithful parents.

Soon after graduating from Eastern Alamance High School in 1973, she began working for the federal government for the Internal Revenue Service.

"My job was being taken over by computers. I was in the Coast Guard Reserve at the time, so I went on active duty in Washington, D.C.," she said, landing a Yeoman's post working in the personnel department.

"I was in a place where I knew nobody. It was a big city, and I was trying to find a church, but it wasn't like it is today where you can Google everything. Looking in the Yellow Pages, I couldn't tell what was close," she said.

Eventually, she just abandoned the idea of finding a church family. After all, her Coast Guard mates didn't go to church, so it didn't fit her lifestyle at the time.

"They were drinkers. It started out just going to have a few drinks," she said.

The job took her around the country to different posts, first landing in Mobile, Alabama, where she met and married fellow Coast Guard member, Dave, in 1982.

"The lifestyle was a lot of partying. That's what the majority of the people did. It was just easier to go along with people. You get unhappy, and you get in that rut," she reflected on that time.

Her travels took her to a stint on Governor's Island, New York. She didn't care for it much, other than the cool attractions like the Statue of Liberty and always being able to get her bearings back then by looking up and seeing the twin towers of the World Trade Center.

She shipped out to sea while stationed in New Bedford, Massachusetts. Then it was on to Kodiak, Alaska, with its remote wilderness areas, short summers and long, dark winters. That's where she retired after 22 years with the Coast Guard in 2000. And it's where her drinking and mental health deteriorated.

The marriage held together, barely. Then Dave, also in the Coast Guard, got stationed in Elizabeth City, North Carolina.

"I went with him, but our marriage got worse. A lot of it had to do with alcohol. I was using it because I wasn't' happy, and it was easier to use it to forget and to self-medicate to sleep at night," she said.

But Dave reached his limit.

"When we got back to North Carolina, eventually, he took me back to my parents (in Mebane). He said, 'Here. You can have her back,'" she said with half a laugh.

Dejected and depressed, she holed up in her childhood bedroom in her parents' house.

"I wasn't being very nice, especially to my mom. I knew I needed help, because I would try to stop drinking, but just couldn't. I knew I needed to get away from where I was," she said.

Her pastor told her about the Durham Rescue Mission, and called to ask if they had room for her. There's always room for one more, the Mission staff encouraged.

"I knew I needed to be there, but didn't really want to be there," she said of the struggle to stay.

She made an effort. She got accepted to the Victory Program, which helped her get back into studying the Bible. She started mending her relationship with Dave, and they started talking again. They eventually divorced in 2012, but remain good friends.

Relapsing and Then Renewing Her Faith

"I made peace with the Lord. Still, I was almost through with the Victory Program, and something made me mad. I decided I didn't need to be there anymore. When I got back, they told me to sleep it off," she said

As she went back through the Victory Program classes again, "I did pray and ask the Lord to forgive me," she said.

"On one side, you have Satan telling you you're not worthy—and, of course, we're not worthy. But the biggest problem I had was I couldn't forgive myself."

That's when she walked out in the garden at the Good Samaritan Inn and had her "little" chat with God.

"That was the big turnaround for me," she said.

Temps to the Rescue got her a job working for the Durham County Fire Marshal/Emergency Management office. They'd had another Victory Program graduate who had worked out well, so they thought with her military experience, it would be a good fit.

And it was. At age 55, she was dreading—but fully expecting—stereotypical age discrimination or to hear, "you're overqualified" in response to her job search. Temps to the Rescue had the relationships she needed to start building her own. She started a new career, alcohol free, doing fulfilling work she loved.

It was hard work. During an emergency, the team was "there for the duration," she said, working seven days a week, 12- to 14-hour shifts. It was rewarding, though, because she knew she was helping people.

"I really enjoyed it," she said.

The biggest challenge after graduating from the Mission's Victory Program was her fear of coming home and being around the same people who led to her unhappiness, she said.

"I didn't know if I was strong enough. I found a place in Durham and had a lease on my own for a year before moving back to Mebane," she said.

Having repaired her friendship with her ex-husband, Dave stored her things at his house in Tyner while she got on her feet at the Mission. He and his new partner were going to be out of town, but told her she could come over and pack her things to take home with her.

"I go in and there on the counter was a bottle of wine and a bottle of liquor," she said. "I said, 'Oh no,' and I just froze. I couldn't move. I was going to call somebody at the Mission just to have somebody talk to me, but there was no (cell) service out there. There was a house phone, but no phone book. I knew Dave would never do anything to make me fall, because he was doing everything he could to help me. I was just in shock."

Feeling panicked, she was trying to think of a church to call "I didn't care if they thought I was crazy, I was just trying to find someone to pray for me. However, with no phone book she didn't have that option.

"Then I got the devil on one shoulder, sitting there talking to me. 'Just have a drink and relax. You can start packing that stuff up later.' I said, 'God will know,' and the devil says, 'Don't worry, God will forgive you.' I said, 'But God doesn't want us to keep repeating the same mistakes over and over. I'm here all alone, not knowing what to do.'

Shelia Joyce's father

"And then it was like I heard gentle voice: 'Shelia, you're not alone, I'm here with you.'"

∽∾

She Stopped Panicking and Started Packing

∽∾

"Any desire for alcohol just went away," she said. "For the longest time after that, just being around it, the smell of it, made me want to throw up. I went around the house and packed up."

In 2013, she moved back into her grandmother's house after a year of living on her own in Durham. This was the trial she'd dreaded, being around the same influences, worrying she'd fall back into the old patterns from her youth.

That same year, her dad died. He had dementia, but before he declined, he knew she'd come back to the Lord, which made her happy because they were close.

"People thought if anything would make me go back to drinking, it would be losing my dad, but I didn't fall because I didn't want to disappoint him again," she said.

As a safety net during that time, for a while, she'd ask her mom to call her 15 minutes after arriving at a gathering so she'd have an excuse to leave if she felt her sobriety was fragile, didn't feel up to it or thought there would be a lot of drinking. She didn't need those calls after a while, and her work and church life were going smoothly.

She likes to tell the story of how in 2016, a revival came to nearby Burlington, and she found her voice for leading others to Christ. The revival got so big, it outgrew New Hope Baptist Church and the Fire Marshal (her agency!) stepped in, so they moved to a tent.

Shelia Joyce

"I'd be so tired at end of day, I'd ask myself, 'Do I really want to go,' but then I'd go. I'm there one night, and they were asking for altar workers, and I thought it would be so great to be able to lead people to Christ, but I wasn't ready."

She said she felt a physical "shove" on her back, and was going to ask her brother, who was with her, to stop that. But then she realized her brother was standing in front of her, and when she turned around, nobody was there.

"I said, 'Okay, God, I got the message,'" she said, taking it as a sign that she should be an altar worker. She realized her doubts were holding her back because she didn't feel worthy.

"Then a woman (at the revival) said to me, 'God would never want me back, you wouldn't understand.' I said, 'Let me tell you a story.' The woman said, 'You do understand.'

"He does want you back and He will welcome you with open arms," Joyce said.

She said she's seen so many people turn their lives around because of the Durham Rescue Mission and the faith Ernie and Gail Mills had to build it.

Now retired once more after eight years at her Emergency Management job in Durham, Joyce serves on the Mission's Temps to the Rescue Board. Since most people hired through the agency are Durham Rescue Mission clients, she is a voice of a person who's been through the program.

"Sometimes, these people, they need somebody to hold their hand and sit down and help them learn this stuff, to help them get started so they don't feel like quitting. A lot of these people have been very heavy into alcohol and drugs their entire lives. They really need someone in there to teach them and show them and give them the motivation to do it, too," she said.

And sometimes, she said, "People just need somebody to give them validation and make them feel like they're worthy or wanted. That's what the Mission does, makes you feel like you're worthy and you do matter."

CHAPTER
Eight

Reclaiming Lost Childhood,
Reframing the Future

Unike Bankhead didn't even know if she'd have a place to stay when she planned to take her two little girls on the 2 a.m. bus to Durham, North Carolina from Columbus, Ohio.

All she knew was she had to keep it a secret so she and her children Zanya, 6, Zi'onna, 4 at the time, could safely escape the toxic cycle of poverty and abuse that plagued their lives for the previous six years.

She couldn't call her mother. She did tell her daughter's special education teacher, a person with whom she'd become friends through caring for little Zanya. Zanya has cerebral palsy, a brain disorder that causes motor function challenges. Bankhead wanted to let the teacher know they were leaving, but the teacher didn't just help her prepare; she purchased the bus tickets for her and her two girls and made sure they made it to the bus station on time.

"I only had $200, and I was going to use it to buy our tickets. She bought the tickets for us," Bankhead said, still in awe of the teacher's kindness because she knew of their circumstances and living in the "worst, most dangerous apartments Columbus, Ohio had to offer."

She and the children made it to the station, but then the bus had technical difficulties and didn't leave until 5 a.m. It didn't reach North

Carolina until 9 p.m., making it a 20-plus-hour odyssey for her and the girls. Bankhead was determined to make the journey. She was out of options and homeless. If she wasn't on this bus, she'd probably be riding a city bus trying to stay warm until they could find a place to stop.

A Life Changing Decision

The one thing Bankhead clung to was a line she read on the Durham Rescue Mission website that said, "It brings you closer to God." She didn't have much direction growing up, but she remembered her grandmother sharing scripture and wanted to know more. She was 23 but felt like a lost little girl with two little girls of her own to protect.

"I was willing to do anything at that time, not knowing if the Durham Rescue Mission could take me. I just had to have faith," she said.

As it so happened, the Mission did have room at the inn—the Good Samaritan Inn—shelter for women and families. And she was just in time. It was January, 2020. If she had made the decision two months later, the doors might have been closed due to the COVID-19 pandemic.

Back in high school in Lorain, Ohio, life wasn't exactly easy after her dad died when she was 12. However, the future looked bright for the talented, well-rounded student. She got good grades, played three sports, and was on the dance team in high school. With an emotionally distant mother, though, Bankhead had little support or foundation to learn right from wrong, she said, other than from her grandmother, who tried.

At 16, her troubles began when she met a boy, and soon she dropped out of school with a tenth-grade education. She had her first daughter, Zanya, with him at 16. Still a child herself, she was ill equipped to cope with that, let alone the squalid living conditions, poverty and episodes of violence that followed.

Finding Rest: From Nowhere to Turn to Turning Her Life Around

Once settled at the Good Samaritan Inn, life settled down for Bankhead and the children.

Unike Bankhead's daughters Zi'onna and Zanya

Unike Bankhead

"I found rest. It was the first time in years I was able to sleep from sundown to sunup. It created a lot of structure for me that I never had bouncing from house to house. I was never able to keep anything— losing clothes, my phone always off. Here I could start building a foundation for my life and my kids' lives—of what our future could look like," Bankhead said.

Bankhead started making a list of things she didn't have. From "girly clothes," to remembering long forgotten dreams of going into business or sales, Bankhead restored the things she'd missed out on in childhood.

First on her list was missing out on her high school diploma, so she pursued her General Education Diploma (GED).

"I was so determined, I just studied and worked at nighttime. As soon as they opened the college, I instantly went to get my GED," Bankhead said. She got it on May 7, 2021.

A couple days later, she had a real graduation ceremony, with a cap and gown, as she completed the Victory Program at the Mission.

With her training from the program, she became a data entry clerk at the Mission and was soon hired full-time on staff in 2023.

She got to experience milestones she missed out on in her traumatic youth, like getting her driver's license (at age 25) and her first car.

She understands when clients want to leave the Mission early. Something makes them mad, or they are ready for more independence. But she advises them to stay the course.

'Don't Settle.'

"Don't settle. Don't limit your vision. It's all how you talk about yourself. I had to change the way I dress. I never was taught how to be

Unike Bankhead at the 2023 Durham Rescue Mission Fall Fundraising Banquet

a woman. Living how I was living, I was mad and angry. Being able to sit still, I got the lesson," Bankhead said.

Her daughters are thriving in school, with her eldest receiving speech therapy twice a week, and is using a speech device to communicate. They also attend the Mission's daycare program. The confidence she's gained at the Mission has helped Bankhead be a better advocate for her daughter's disability.

"Me being at the Durham Rescue Mission made it a lot easier for me to accomplish anything," she said.

Growing up in such chaos and being thrust into such precarious circumstances with so much responsibility at a young age, Bankhead said she never learned what a "good life" was like.

The support of the Mission allowed her to get stronger on her feet and mature in her relationship with Jesus Christ, Bankhead said. She sees the possibilities before her and how to help her children thrive—instead of just trying to survive.

"The Durham Rescue Mission created a family for me—people and friends I can talk to, cry to if I need to. They gave me a different outlook on life. Unless you know my starting point, you would never know my gratitude for all of that," Bankhead said. "Being at the Durham Rescue Mission gave me the courage to keep trying."

She is learning to quiet the chaos and wait for God to tell her when she is ready for the next step, instead of jumping from one thing to another as she was conditioned to do growing up.

Bankhead took a picture of herself the day she entered the Durham Rescue Mission, determined that when she left, she would be changed.

"I am 27. I grew up in this place. I'm creating my own identity in this place, building it brick by brick," she said. "I know I am so different than the person who walked in."

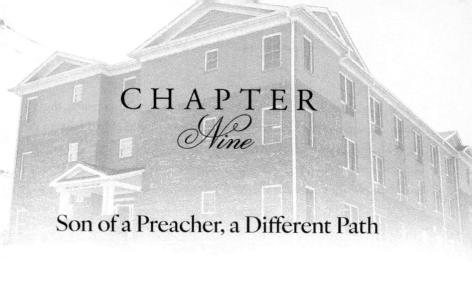

CHAPTER
Nine

Son of a Preacher, a Different Path

When Ernie Mills called his son and namesake, Ernie Mills Jr. and asked him to meet him at the IHOP at 5 a.m., the younger Mills knew it would be more than just enjoying a nostalgic stack of tasty buttermilk pancakes with his dad.

"I mean, he's an early riser, sure, but for him to ask me to meet like that, I knew he wanted to talk to me about something important, or he needed my help," he said.

That's why he tried not to laugh when his father asked him to come head up the Development Office at the Mission. Rev. Mills was offering his son a salary that was 30 percent of what he earned the previous year in his real estate business.

Besides, he told his father, "I've never been a fundraiser before. Why would you want me to do that?"

"I think you're the man for the job," the pastor insisted, telling him his success in real estate was proof enough he could do what he was asking for the Mission. "I need to know Monday because we must hire someone soon. Things are growing so fast."

It was Thursday, so the son had just a few days to consider the major life change his father was asking him to make. He'd have to talk to his wife, Denise, he decided.

He figured he'd pull out the tax documents and show her the numbers, so she could see the 70% pay cut.

Turning Point

"I wrote down what I made the year before on one card, and what Daddy could pay me on another one. When she came in, I said, 'Sweetheart, here's what happened,' and slid the cards over to her on the table," he said.

Ernie Jr. and Denise at the 2023 Durham Rescue Mission Fall Fundraising Banquet

"She swept them away - never looking at them. Instead, she leaned across the table, grabbed my hands, looked straight into my eyes, and asked, 'What does God want you to do?'"

"All of that will take care of itself if you're doing what God wants you to do," she said, her response taking him by surprise.

"I started crying. I wanted her to say no. I was such a coward that I wanted her to say we can't do that. I still hadn't reached that point of surrender. When she said those words—that's when I surrendered for the first time in my life. I knew at that moment I was going to do what God wanted me to do. I'd been running for so long," he said.

Being raised in the church, growing up with his mother and father running the Mission, he wasn't exactly a stereotypical rebellious preacher's kid, or one to follow in his father's footsteps. Ernie Jr. said he'd been trying to live life his own way, not how God wanted.

"I wasn't fulfilled. At 3 o'clock in the morning—when you wake up in the middle of the night—I didn't have that feeling of peace," he explained.

Fighting 'Misdeeds' Brings Roots Full-Circle

First, as a young man, he chose a career in law enforcement, where he thought he'd be doing what he felt called to do—help the little guy and defend the defenseless.

He served in the Durham County Sherriff's Office for a decade. Funny, though, when he talks about his most memorable and meaningful accomplishment, it's not arresting criminals that comes to mind.

In a bit of a full-circle event, it was the work he did on a case involving someone losing their home. His investigation involved both the theme he'd grown up with working with people who had no home, as well as his future real estate expertise. He found himself investigating how a frail, little old lady had the deed to her home swindled away from her.

That story made the local TV news, he recalls.

An elderly woman with failing eyesight was duped by Quit Claim deed scammers. Pretending to do home repairs, a pair of unscrupulous men tricked her into signing her house deed over to them.

That situation made then-Deputy Sherriff Ernie Mills Jr. angry. He was so mad, he said he could only play bad cop-bad cop in his office where he had the victim and the man who now held the deed sitting before him that day. He tossed the police file toward the man. He all but shouted at the man, "When I get back, she better be smiling, or you're going to jail," and stormed out of his own office.

Sure enough, by the time he returned, the lady was indeed smiling. The man agreed to sign the deed back over to the rightful owner. Once the paperwork was filed with the Register of Deeds, Ernie Jr. wanted to be the one to deliver it in person to her door. That's when the news station got wind of the story and came along for the ride.

"I had tons of arrests, where people were wanted for terrible crimes and even murder. But if I had to look back and choose my greatest achievement, it would probably be that. She didn't understand what had happened. They were just telling her she had to pay rent on the house where she'd lived and raised her children," he said.

He was determined to hand her back the deed to her own home she'd lost through trickery. It was the most fulfilling moment of his law enforcement career.

Meeting Denise

While working for the Sheriff's Office had its meaningful moments, he didn't have the peace he spoke of. He worked in law enforcement full time from 1997 to 2007.

He persevered, and the couple married in 2009. He loves telling the story of how they met. It's like an endearing scene from a Hallmark movie.

Denise was the activities director at a nursing home and was holding a Cinco de Mayo celebration. Ernie was at the nursing home on official business to inspect the facility on behalf of the Sheriff's Office.

Ernie Jr. served as a deputy for the Durham County Sheriff's Office.

Ernie Jr. with his parents at a Greater Durham Chamber of Commerce event

"She was speaking Spanish and wearing a sombrero," and it seemed everywhere he went to inspect, there would be Denise, checking on a nursing home resident or checking in with staff.

While walking past the rose garden courtyard in the middle of the nursing home, Ernie asked her if she took care of those roses.

"No, is there a problem?" she replied, knowing he was there to inspect the premises.

"There's no problem," Ernie said. "I was just thinking the roses are almost a beautiful as you are."

She smiled and rolled her eyes, walking away. But, as he was leaving out the front door after completing his inspection, he heard her call out to him.

"Excuse me, sir," and she handed him a fistful of those roses.

A few weeks later, Ernie ran into one of Denise's coworkers, who recognized him from doing the inspection. Ernie Jr. gave him his card to pass along to Denise.

Now, he was in a relationship with a beautiful and talented young lady who became the love of his life, but something was still missing, he said.

"So, I thought, 'Well, I just need to make more money. I've got friends that have boats and RVs. Maybe I need more money?' I went to night school and got my real estate license and opened my own business. God allowed me to prosper," in real estate, while still working for the Sherriff's Office, he said.

He was good at the real estate business, and he enjoyed doing it.

But money didn't fill that void, either. "I didn't have the peace that I was doing what God wanted me to do," he said.

∽◦◠

His Own Way Gives Way to God's Way

◡◠◡

"I was trying to live Ernie's way. Ya know, from way back, people would ask me what I wanted to do when I grew up. Do you want to be just like your daddy? The answer was, no! I was tired of being Ernie Jr. I didn't want to have to live up to that. I thought someday I want someone to come up to my dad and say, 'Aren't you Ernie's dad?' But from early on, I was running from what God wanted me to do," he admits.

"I wanted to be a good man. Respectable, honorable. When you work in law enforcement, it's sure not about the money. I wanted to fight for the little man. Those who couldn't fight for themselves," he said.

"In law enforcement, I was able to achieve my goals of helping the helpless and fighting for the weak," he said. "And in real estate, I was able to negotiate good terms for my clients."

But he still felt he wasn't doing what God wanted.

Fast forward to that improbable request from his father when Denise, his wife by that time, asked him that all-important question about what God wanted him to do.

The excitement and adrenaline rush of law enforcement didn't make him happy. The money from real estate didn't fulfill him. Suddenly he knew why Denise's question weighed so heavily and the answer was clear.

Soon, he sold his RV that he'd loved to take to watch NASCAR races with his season tickets at Bristol Motor Speedway in Tennessee. He'd paid cash for that RV with his real estate income. But he couldn't afford to keep it on the Mission salary and wouldn't have the flexible vacation time he had as his own boss in real estate. His dad was offering just one week of vacation.

Next, he put his shiny metallic blue decked out Ford F-350 pickup truck up for sale, trading it in for a 1990 Jeep. He'd paid cash for that shiny truck, too, and didn't have payments, but he knew he needed to put money aside if he was taking such a large pay cut.

"I feel like financially, I went way backwards. It didn't make any rational sense to do what I did. But, fast forward a few months to our anniversary that year," he said, and what he gained can't be measured.

The couple decided they'd stay home and order pizza and watch a movie instead of spending a lot of money. "She said, 'That's wonderful,'" he said.

"The morning of our anniversary, she had her hand behind her back, and said she had something for me. I said, 'Stop, we promised no gifts!' She brought her hand around, and we were expecting our first child," he said.

The news came after Ernie started the new job at the Mission, and he credits his journey and God for the blessings. The couple had discussed adoption following the lengthy failed fertility treatments, and then finally taking a break from trying because of all the painful disappointments.

"God allowed her to have a perfect pregnancy and delivery, and stay home with Peyton," their daughter, he said, which meant a 100 percent pay cut for her. By their next anniversary, the plan was pizza and a movie again, and Denise had another surprise; she was expecting their second child. Ernie Mills, III, whom they call Trace, who was born two days before Peyton's first birthday. A few years later, they had another son, Levi.

"When I look at my family, I'm amazed. Through all this twisted and winding road, God preserved me. Times I should have been killed in law enforcement, alone and outnumbered on a dark road, but God preserved me," he said.

The Most Generous Partners

As the Vice President of Development for the Mission, he reaches out to supporters who've indicated they want to partner with the Mission, telling stories of how the Mission has changed lives. How people who were a nuisance or burden in society, who are now employed, homeowners, good neighbors, who themselves often donate back to the Mission.

"You're not going to get a cold call, telemarketer kind of conversation with us. It's people who raised their hands as wanting to partner with us. That's a huge vote of confidence, out of their limited resources," he said.

"They're not buying a product they're going to take home and use. They are giving of their money to create a product hopefully they'll never have to use. I get to work with the most generous people on the planet!

"I went from asking people to give $100 and then $600 to sponsor a day at our lady's campus to $500,000, and then a $1 million for building a dorm," he said.

That $1 million donation came with a catch that was close to home for Mills. A local couple challenged him to raise $1 million within a year and they would match it dollar for dollar to help pay for construction of the new Mills Family Student Housing, to be named in honor of his parents, who were stepping down from their leadership roles into fundraising roles at the time.

"Do you think you can do it," the couple asked.

"We've never done it before, but if God put it on your heart to challenge me that way, I can do it," he assured the couple, who kept their donation anonymous.

When he called to let them know he'd met the goal, they asked him to come by their house to pick up the matching check.

"They were both shaking with excitement, like a child going to Disney for the first time.

They handed me a regular handwritten check that was torn out of a checkbook. The wife said, 'My 401K in heaven just got so much bigger!'"

"We have so many fantastic partners. I work with the most generous people on the planet," he said.

From starting as a staff of one, Ernie Mills Jr. now manages 20 people. Most of those were former clients. None are professional fundraisers, but their compelling stories touch people through authentic and genuine connections and faith, he said.

"It's just people who were willing to say, 'Hey, God, can you use me?' We are testament to the fact that God has taken weak and simple things to completely confound conventional wisdom," he said.

"Several times a year, we have people come to look at our systems from other missions and associations," he said. It struck him when someone from the Winston-Salem Rescue Mission—the place where his father got his start—came for a tour to get help with their fundraising.

"They came here, and they said we want to be like the Durham Rescue Mission when we grow up," he said. "Our roots are there, yet God has blessed us, and they're here learning from us."

"Now, I see a lot of the same people I would have been arresting who are coming here to find 'a rest' from the storms of life," he said.

"Instead of just going to jail, they are finding rejuvenation in a new way of life, living a clean, sober and productive life," which is what is most rewarding for him.

"It's that purpose I was searching for. I feel fulfilled. I love to tell stories, and that's really my job here," he said.

"Of course, I have all new headaches," he laughed. But he wouldn't have it any other way.

CHAPTER
Ten

A Winding Road to Redemption

For my thoughts are not your thoughts,
neither are your ways my ways,
declares the LORD.

As the heavens are higher than the earth,
so are my ways higher than your ways
and my thoughts than your thoughts.

—Isaiah 55:8–9

Personal injury attorneys call California State Route 99 the "Highway to Hell" because of its reputation as the most dangerous highway in America.

For Ward Gillett, it was the beginning of his Damascus road experience, the turning point for his salvation—though the path was winding and long.

It was the fall of 1993, and the 30-year-old Gillett just had a major disagreement and falling out with the door-to-door magazine sales crew he was traveling with. He threw his things in his bag, figuratively thumbed his nose at his ex-bosses and literally stuck his thumb in the air to head south out of Bakersfield, with the idea of heading home to New York.

He made his way to State Route 99, a vestigial portion of the iconic former US Highway 99, which originally cut through the center of California as the primary north-south highway starting in 1926 until 1972 when it was decommissioned. Sections that are left suffer from outdated engineering and the one Gillett traveled that day in 1993 ranks consistently on the annual list of most fatalities per 100 miles.

A trucker picked up Gillett, and as the 161 miles down the middle of the state sped by to Rialto, where the trucker lived, the rider and driver spoke amiably for the 2½-hour trip.

"We started talking about Jesus. The truck driver told me his story. So, when we got to Rialto, I asked if he needed help unloading the truck. He asked me to go to his church that Sunday. I went, and first I heard testimony of the pastor. I went back and heard the testimony of a converted Muslim," Gillett said.

Gillett felt the spirit move him, and accepted Jesus as his Lord and Savior that day.

But, said Gillett, the next 14 years were like, "wandering in the wilderness," because he couldn't make the changes he knew God wanted him to make. Sure, outwardly, his language and cussing cleaned up. But not much else changed.

"There were a whole lot of things going on in my life. I was dealing with drugs—cocaine was my drug of choice—and alcohol. I also had a lot of anger, resentment and bitterness," he said.

Fourteen years after getting saved, then losing his way, Gillett found his way to the Durham Rescue Mission. It took him getting there to look back and understand the journey he'd been on long before that drive down State Route 99 to Rialto to where he first found out about Jesus.

Mother's Abandonment, Father's Death

When Gillett was born in 1963 in Rome, New York, his father was in and out of the hospital with cancer, and his mother abandoned him and his older sister, Bonnie. From birth, he, along with his sister, was placed in foster care with a childless couple, Herbert and Gladys Gillett, who eventually adopted them.

His adoption at age 13 caused upheaval for Gillett. Until then, he was the namesake of his biological father, Ward McAllister, who died from the cancer when young Ward was just two. The adoption meant changing his name to Gillett, and the growing adolescent struggled with the change to his identity. He was a 13-year-old likely dealing with feelings of loss and resurfaced abandonment issues from his biological mother whom he never knew, either.

"I didn't want to take on their last name. I was making a name for myself in baseball, McCallister. I was resentful. I wasn't angry at them for adopting me. I just had plans. I had dreams, aspirations. I don't blame those things for what I did, though," he said.

The Gilletts were good Christians who brought him up as best they could to know better than what he did. "I just didn't understand a lot of things," he said

On his last day of high school before graduation in 1982, he shipped out to basic training in the Army, a decision he'd made in 11th grade—and ultimately a decision that didn't fit well with his rebellious nature—what he calls his "attitude problem and anger issue."

In 1985, his adoptive mother, Gladys Gillett, died, increasing his feelings of rejection.

∽∾

From Adoption to Addiction: Pillar to Post—
a Peripatetic Road to Ruin

∽∾

A few years later, after he left the Army and began work as a traveling salesman, he began to drink and use cocaine heavily as he tried to escape his lifelong anger and abandonment issues.

"The traveling sales business is filled with a lot of drugs and promiscuity. I was searching for love in the wrong places trying to fill a void that could never be satisfied in this world," he said.

His addiction led him to choosing to hang out with the wrong people in the wrong environments, resulting in bad decisions and arrests for DUI's and imprisonments.

Ward Gillette graduating from Tabernacle Baptist College in Greenville, SC

"I was seeking making a million dollars as a salesman," he said, constantly crisscrossing the country, selling everything from cars to carpets, from jewelry to Amway to magazines.

"I can't express the road of debauchery I went down. I did what I had to do to accomplish what I wanted," he said.

In 1996, his adoptive father, Herbert, died. Although Gillett by then experienced trusting the Lord, as he put it, he wasn't living his life in a biblical way, and the loss of Herbert was another blow. It increased his self-destructive behavior and compounded lifelong feelings of rejection.

In 1997, he met and fell in love with a woman named Gloria. Their on-again-off-again tumultuous relationship was marked by a substance-abuse lifestyle. He even spent time in jail because she accused him of domestic abuse, of which he was found not guilty, he said.

"I spent 45 days in jail. In that time, I lost my job. I lost my apartment. I even lost my dog—there's a Western album there somewhere," he joked.

After that, he began attending church and tried to pull his life together. The couple reconciled and got engaged in 2001, with plans for a more stable life including a move from Arizona to Minnesota.

"We were to meet for breakfast on a Monday morning. I spoke to her last on Saturday evening and told her I loved her. That Monday I went to where we were to meet. As I was sitting there, I heard some employees talking, and this is when I heard that Gloria was killed in a car accident and died Sunday morning at Duluth Hospital," he said.

His emotions ran the gamut from anger at the events to trusting the Lord—for a time, anyway. It didn't last. After about a year, he became discouraged, he said, and reverted to his old ways.

That's when he moved to North Carolina in 2002. Still heavily using cocaine, he drifted in and out of jobs and homelessness. From

Ward with pastors from Navajo Baptist Temple in Shiprock, NM

2005 to 2006, he attended the Richmond (Virginia) Outreach Center ministry for eight months, and then moved to Wilson, North Carolina, after finishing the program.

In October 2007, still struggling with his problems, living in what he calls a "one-room flop house on Lee Street," in Wilson, Gillett had had enough of himself and was about to give up hope.

Answered Prayers: The Durham Rescue Mission

"While I was in that room praying, I got a knock on my door, and it was the assistant pastor and his wife from Bethel Baptist Church in Wilson, where I was attending. They prayed with me. Two weeks later, after Sunday morning services, they drove me down to the Durham Rescue Mission," about an hour-and-a-half away, he said.

"I had a need and it was spiritual," Gillett said. From the minute he entered the Durham Rescue Mission, he realized things would be different. He was approved to attend the Victory Program, eventually becoming a supervisor of the Men's Division at the Mission, under the guidance of the Mission pastors.

"That was the overhaul of my life, coming to the Durham Rescue Mission. It was a total change," Gillett said. "The first song I heard them sing was 'Victory in Jesus,' and it truly is."

In 2009, he moved back to Wilson just as his friends, Pastor Beckles and his wife, were leaving the Bethel Baptist Youth ministry for another church. Gillett became youth minister, where he served for four years.

"The Lord was preparing me. After that, I moved to Greenville, South Carolina and attended Tabernacle Baptist College."

Just how he was going to pay tuition was another matter. It was 2013, and he was 50 years old. He didn't have a job, but he did have a commanding, deep, resonant voice. Perhaps that's why the secretary of the school's WTBI radio station asked him if he'd ever considered radio ministry.

"I said, no, but I'll pray about it. I cut a tape and filled out an application," and soon he was sharing the gospel and introducing sponsors.

Nerve wracking at first, he soon learned the main key to success was to be himself. As much as he drew on his sales experience for his speaking abilities and stage presence, his confidence came from his faith, he said, and being authentic.

He thinks it's God's sense of humor that back when he was selling magazines door to door, one of his made-up "spiels" was telling people he was a Syracuse University graduate student supporting his degree in communications. "I made that up. I was terrible. I find it ironic I've been doing this for 11 years at WTBI."

As the oldest student in his classes, he found himself being something of an inspiration to younger ministry students. He advised them to start out in youth ministry, as he did, "because we have to learn to reach the young people."

He was active in homeless ministries, to which he could strongly relate. He had several nursing home ministries as well, as he encouraged the younger students to do so, and to always remember the purpose was sharing the gospel.

Ward working at WTBI in Greenville, SC

From Traveling Salesman to Mission Trips

He graduated in the spring of 2018 with bachelor's degree in theology. All the while, he was taking mission trips and was particularly taken with missions to Arizona and working with Native American tribes.

"Every time I'd go through a place called Holbrook, Arizona, I would hear the Lord say He'd like to put a church there," Gillett said.

In 2022, he preached and handed out Bibles while walking in the Navajo festival parade, attended by 250,000 people. "On my way back, I came back through Holbrook, and it was really on my heart to plant a church there," he said.

Before he knew it, he was applying to the local Mission Board to do just that.

"I got ordained December 20, 2023, and the second week of January 2024 I started my deputation to go to churches to raise money to plant a church in Holbrook," Gillett said.

Looking back on that winding road that led to God burdening his heart to plant a church in Arizona, Gillett said he doesn't look back on those "wasted years" with regret.

"I wouldn't change nothin' for nothin,'" he said. "God used all this stuff for good, even in the midst of my wretchedness and sin."

Gillett, with his years of experience in sales, ministry and radio, said, "I know no strangers."

"The Lord works behind the scenes. First of all, all men will come to repentance. My dad died when I was two, and my mother abandoned me. That wasn't my fault. God knew all about that.

He put me in a Christian home," he said.

"I'm blessed. I stand amazed that He put up with me. Before I surrendered, I was so full of myself and wanted to do what I wanted to do. When discouragement came or somebody ticked me off, I was vengeful.

"It was God who brought me to a place called an 'end,' and I thank the Lord He did that, when I was in my bedroom on Lee Street in Wilson. I'd have died without knowing my reward in heaven," he said.

"For 14 years, for Him to put up with me—I was in situations at times I should have been dead. But God was there protecting me. He brought me to the Durham Rescue Mission that October. And that's when I walked into the chapel and I heard all those men singing Victory in Jesus. That was the grace of God reaching out for me."

> *The blessing of the LORD, it maketh rich, and he addeth no sorrow with it."*
>
> **—Proverbs 10:22**

CHAPTER
Eleven

'High Life' Was a Bluff
for Lowlife Existence

Mission Turns Tables on Gambling and Drug Addiction

Reid Beasley remembers a time when he didn't know if his older brother Gary was dead or alive. Reid knew Gary wasn't someone he could trust around his young family. Yet, he still worried about Gary's welfare.

"He wasn't a mean person. He just made some bad choices," the younger Beasley said.

That's an understatement, said Gary Beasley about his "riotous" untrustworthy former self.

"I just really messed up my life. I was definitely a liar. I really spun out of control. I was a gambler. I was an excessive partier. I tried heroin. I tried cocaine. I lived a riotous life—not one that I was proud of," he said.

The two—who later became inseparable since their lives came back together through the Durham Rescue Mission—drifted apart after the death of their mother in 1982 and then their father in 1986. Their dad died with numerous complications, including congestive heart failure, emphysema and asthma.

"I always worked for my dad. My dad was an alcoholic, and while we were working and I was helping him get more accomplished, it seemed like he didn't drink as much. When he passed away, I just didn't care as much," Gary explained about how his motivation shifted toward the family construction company when his father died.

After losing his dad, Gary ditched the business his dad had trained him in and started travelling around the country with his self-taught golf swing. He joined amateur tournaments and rubbing shoulders with celebrities on the circuit, including O.J. Simpson.

Game on! A Gift for Golfing, Gambling, Grift

Gary took his natural golf and gambling handicapping talents around the country, from Las Vegas to Atlantic City to Florida and parts in between.

Along the way, he acquired some less than wholesome skills and habits through his associations, which meant he was always able to make money, even six figures.

"I let money be in charge. When you can walk into a place and buy everybody drinks, I thought it made me feel important," he said. "The right word would be foolish."

By 2001, Gary was 47 and knew it was time for a change. The unhealthy lifestyle of constant partying and drugs caught up with him, taking a toll on his physical, mental and emotional well-being. He decided he should go back home and make a change. He called Reid, who still lived in Durham, to ask for a place to stay while he got back on his feet.

Not His Wayward Brother's Keeper—
But He Knew Where to Get Him Help.

As much as he wanted to help, when Reid got the call from his long-lost brother Gary in November 2001 asking if he could come stay with him, he had to put his young family first.

"I had a newborn. That wasn't going to work," Reid said. Reid was a long-time volunteer at the Mission through Fellowship Baptist Church in Durham. He dropped Gary off at the Mission, knowing the Mission could help him.

Gary and Nancie Beasley on their wedding day

"Reid made this statement to his wife that night," Gary recalled. "He said he knew he could sleep that night because he finally knew I was OK. I'll be forever grateful for what he did."

Grateful though he was, Gary never planned to stay long. He didn't think he needed to. He does remember the Mission made a strong impression on him. Once, during a big ice storm that December, a month into his stay, Gail and Ernie Mills handed him several hundred dollars. They asked him to go buy some kerosene because the Mission lost power and they needed it for the stoves.

"I wouldn't have trusted me with that money the way I'd been living my life," he said. Although he had to go to several places because some stores were out of stock, he did return with the containers, and even handed back the change, he said.

He started to feel he was really turning his life around. After five weeks at the Mission, he got a job offer in January 2002 making $600 a week, plus bonuses.

"I thought the Lord gave me a job, and I got a place to stay. So, I left the Mission. That lasted three or four months. It didn't work out. I came back to the Mission in May 2002 because I was worse than I was the first time," Gary said.

The second time, he stayed, faced his problems, and was accepted to the Victory Program.

"I could see I was doing so much better. I went from basically a blight on society to a fully functioning member of society," he said. "The main thing, through the Victory Program, is learning about the Bible. It gave me hope for the future."

He was given jobs at the Mission, first working on the phone desk and then working in the Men's Division supervisor's office. Still, his plan was not to stay at the Mission. God, it would seem, had other plans.

"When I graduated from the Victory Program, I was the lead supervisor for the Men's Division. All of the sudden, something happened in Temps to the Rescue," he said.

Beasley was asked to run the Temps to the Rescue agency, which helped connect clients to jobs in the community.

"It was not very profitable at the time. But when I took over, all of a sudden, the calls came in, and Temps started flourishing. All the men here were getting work. All the women were getting work," he said.

He received a lot of credit for the newfound success of the agency, he said, but in truth, "I didn't do anything. It looked like I was just a great success story."

It's proof the Lord has a sense of humor, he said. Gary jokes that it probably took him six months to learn how to copy and paste, and now he's able to turn on the computer by himself.

"A lot of times people want to take credit for something, but I didn't do anything," he stressed.

'Now I Have a Wonderful Life.'

In 2024, 22 years later, he still oversaw Temps to the Rescue, signing more than 100 paychecks a week—along with managing many other Mission functions as Vice-President of Operations for the Mission.

"They kept me. Yeah, now I feel like I give back, not just take," he said.

Looking back, he's amazed at the changes in his life since coming to the Mission.

"I remarried and have a great wife. I bought a home. Back then, I couldn't even manage my own life. Now I've got purpose. I am now closer to my brother than I've ever been. I still have contact with my sister, which I didn't back then," he said.

"I'm not perfect; nowhere near. I just care. I just came from being a riotous person to now I have a wonderful life," he said.

Reid summed up the transformation: "We were estranged for a while. I always prayed for him. I always wanted to have a relationship. I didn't know where he was for years. I knew he was not doing well. When he finally called me and said he'd had enough, staying with me wasn't going to be a match, so I dropped him off at the Durham Rescue Mission.

"Now he's got the keys to my safe, my front door and my alarm code. He never would have had any of those things before he came here," said Reid.

"Without the Durham Rescue Mission, I don't know where he'd be. It gave him the structure he never had before. It gave him accountability and purpose. And he enjoys what he does."

In a full circle moment, Reid retired as a supervisor from UPS in 2015 after 35 years, and Gary asked him to come work at the Mission.

Reid started part time, and then the Mission hired him as director in charge of the thrift stores, Training Center, district managers, and fleet management.

"Gary and I both learned how to manage people from the construction business," he said. Now both work side-by-side at the Mission.

"Now he's given me a purpose," Reid said.

It's interesting to think that now Gary, with all those years of hard living, is likely the oldest living Beasley in the family, Reid said.

"When his life changed, his health changed. He's probably as healthy now as I've ever seen him," Reid said.

Gary agrees. "It's all because of Ernie Mills' vision and the rules they put in place. The rules don't change at the Mission. And that's the best part.

"When you quit doing the things that you've always done, quit going to the locations which caused you trouble—I rid myself of my old 'friends.' I made a lot of money, but it all became an addiction," he said.

"Now, I don't make what I used to make, but I've got more than I've ever had. I honor God. I'm not trying to impress someone. And it all came from my life changing."

Gary knows he wouldn't have his wife, Nancie, whom he credits for much of his success, if he hadn't come to the Mission. "She keeps me going down the correct road."

CHAPTER
Twelve

Game-Changing Training Center

⟨∾⟩

Opening Opportunities for Those Left Out

⟨∾⟩

O nce, while sitting at lunch and chatting, Rob Tart didn't think too much when a Mission client suddenly looked up at him and asked with a bit of awe: "Do you realize I have worked at this job for a whole year."

"I just kept eating lunch, and smiled and nodded," Tart said. "This guy was in his 40s. He said, 'You don't understand. I have never worked at the same job for one year in my life.'"

It was an illustration of what a difference the Mission makes in individual lives by teaching even basic skills, responsibility and accountability. It also convinced Tart more than ever that his idea of having a separate warehouse and training building would not just make the Mission's growing thrift store business more efficient, it would provide more opportunities for clients to learn tasks in ways that worked best for them and build progressively on what they learn.

Tart knew from experience that people that were good at some things within the stores could be "terrible with the customers," which could cause serious setbacks. He wanted to be able to set people with specific needs up for success as much as possible so there was a place for everyone.

A Big Idea: Break it Down into Small Steps

In 2015, Tart proposed something big that would be a game changer for running the thrift stores and ultimately financing the Mission. It would centralize operations and grow the Mission, he reasoned. He wanted to purchase a separate building to coordinate the thrift store operations while supporting other training programs to give clients work experiences.

He wasn't sure what the right size would be. At first, the Mission was looking at 20,000-square-foot spaces, but then the real estate agent they worked with showed them the former Montgomery Ward department store warehouse a few miles from the main Mission campus. The Mission purchased the 88,000-square-foot building at 2425 South Alston Avenue in Durham and started using it for training and donation processing.

Tart admits the Mission Training Center experiment, "didn't start off that great. It just increased expenses at first."

But once the Mission opened a fourth store, that's when the productivity gains started saving the Mission money and grew the profits in the thrift store operation in the long run.

The building gave the Mission space for all the donations that came into the stores. At the centralized center, there was room to sort, organize, price, discard what couldn't be sold, and then distribute items evenly back out to the stores ready for sale. That eased the pressure of all those backroom tasks on the store staff. The building also provided much-needed classroom training space.

"The Durham Rescue Mission Training Center and thrift stores gave so many job opportunities," Tart said, "truck driving, bookkeeping, warehousing, sorting and pricing, cashiering, stocking, managing, and more."

The First Step to One Step at a Time

"I always wanted a warehouse," Tart said, quickly correcting himself and quipping that on the staff of the training center, if you call it a "warehouse," you have to put $20 into jar to buy Krispy Kreme doughnuts for everyone. The point of the Mission Training Center, he said, is to train up clients so they can get on their own two feet.

His idea drew on his early fast-food experience before he went to college for the ministry.

"I knew what the fast-food industry does. They take people with low or no skills, often people with disabilities, basically making a factory back there, and they are productive from Day 1," Tart said.

When he was a teenager, Tart recalled starting out at McDonald's taught him one skill at a time, and from the first day, they were providing value. He watched as it leveled the learning curve for people with developmental delays, learning disabilities, or other challenges, who felt encouraged and empowered by being productive immediately because tasks were broken down into achievable parts.

"They train you on one thing. First, they taught how to dress the bun. Squirt, squirt, holler out for cheese and pickles, and then go to learn the next station. Eventually you become proficient in all the tasks," said Tart, who went on to manage stores and later moved on to the job in Germany managing a Burger King on the PX. He knew what worked for him.

"I took that same model and broke down all the thrift store jobs into parts," Tart said.

That allowed someone with great people-managerial skills to focus on managing a store, versus all the back-end processing parts of the job.

It gave others a place to start out and set them up for success. As an example, Tart described an individual who struggled and seemed overwhelmed with multiple tasks required to work in the thrift stores.

"If you handed him a bag of donations and he had to separate the ladies' clothing from the men's from the children's and decide which

A client working at the Durham Rescue Mission Job Training and Donation Center

was worth selling, or which should be recycled—asking him to make all those decisions—he just couldn't do it," Tart explained.

"We put him over in the Training Center presorting clothing, and he has just thrived. He doesn't have to do 20 things; he just has two or three. He can look at the zippers or see if there are stains or tears. If it's OK, he'll put it where you resell it, and if not, recycle. He doesn't decide prices or sizes or anything else. Just is it worthy to sell?"

"After that, he moved on to grading and separating dresses from pants from blouses. It just seems people can develop a little better learning one at a time instead of 20 steps at once," Tart said.

Workforce Solutions

"When we got to opening the third thrift store, the problem we were having was finding someone who could manage both the production and the retail side of the store. Those are very different skills. It's a highly qualified and sort of rare person that has both, and they're not usually clients at the Rescue Mission," Tart said. "We do our best to hire a former client."

Meanwhile, the Mission leadership was asking Tart to open a fourth store, but he was having challenges keeping managers at the three that were already open.

The Mission Training Center provided the solutions they needed.

"We centralized all the processing so the donations that arrive at a thrift store will end up on a truck for processing, and they'll be shipped back sized, ready for sale, priced. We do as much as we can in that warehouse, making it easier to manage the stores," Tart said.

Clients work the clothing sorting conveyor line to determine if clothes are in good shape to sell.

The Temps to the Rescue program, which was a way to connect Victory Program participants with work experience in the community, grew with the Mission. With the stores and training center, Temps to the Rescue could "find anybody a job," at the Mission, and the thrift stores had a steady stream of workers who could learn new skills, from sorting and pricing donations, managing stores and personnel, and all the jobs in between.

From COVID-19 Setback to 'Tight as a Tick' Solution

Everyone was very glad the Mission purchased the large facility when the COVID-19 pandemic caused so much disruption. For the Mission, the training center building was a saving grace because of all the storage space it provided.

During the pandemic, other charity donation centers completely closed. With the 88,000 square feet, the Mission took all the donations that came in, meeting donors at their homes or wherever they needed.

"We filled up that warehouse tight as a tick and started wholesaling things out," Tart said. "We survived that, but it was a real interesting time."

∽ↄↄↄ

What Happens Inside the Training Center

ↄↄↄ∽

The Mission Training Center makes sense out of the sometimes-chaotic variety of donations that come into the Mission stores. Sometimes it's literally trash and cannot be salvaged.

The community can bring their donations to the local Durham Rescue Mission Thrift Store. Trucks go around to all the stores to pick up the donations on a regular basis and bring them back to the training center for processing.

The waste is removed and the rest that has value and can be resold at the stores is sorted into large roller bins. The Mission clients are instructed on how to price things, depending on the category.

Some clients test electronics. If someone donates a coffee pot, the client staff plug it in to make sure it works. Tart said normally they mark prices at about a third of what the item would cost at retail. When it comes to clothing, items are inspected for things like stains, tears and working zippers.

Unlike other thrift stores, the Mission Thrift Stores puts their clothing items by size on the rack, which improves the shopping experience. It also takes a lot of labor. They can do this because of the efficiencies at the Mission Training Center, he said.

The Mission Training Center became a model for other ministries around the country to tour to learn how to set up successful thrift store operations.

"One of the reasons thrift stores fail is they don't know their pricing philosophy," Tart said. Often, they'll evaluate each item and "try to get every bit of value out of everything they have," he said.

"If they've got a very expensive pair of blue jeans, they'll price them as high as they can, and try for a boutique pricing model," for example. However, this often results in pricing themselves out of their typical market base, Tart said, and takes a lot of time and resources.

On the other end of the spectrum, thrift stores like Goodwill Industries use what's called "menu pricing," he said. That's when there's a sign with shirts, sweaters, and jeans, and customers pay at the register based on that menu price.

"We're kind of in between. We'll try to value it out. But if we can see this is clearly from Walmart, if it's in great shape, we'll try to sell it. Otherwise, we'll recycle it. So, they can choose from three pricing levels for a type of item: Good, Better, Best. Then we have WOW, which might be an item like a 100% leather jacket. But the objective is to mill through the clothing as fast as we can," he said.

"We're trying to have a range of prices the Mission clients who work in the training center can pick from to price items. We know when customers come in, they know how much they can spend," Tart said. "The point is, I don't want to price too high. You gotta decide, 'Is this a ministry.'"

Tart said the thrift store operation makes money for the ministry. To that end, "We believe business is the best educator in the United States," Tart said. For the clientele of the Mission, who are facing challenges managing their lives and often lack formal training, "Those people can learn more at jobs than they can in schools."

"We've got men here who never had a W-2 tax paying job in their whole lives. Many have never had a driver's license. There was no father figure. They just meandered around the neighborhood with no direction," he said.

The Mission and the jobs at the Training Center and thrift stores provide structure so clients know they must be up and dressed at a certain hour and eat at the same time, he said.

"The objective is not to keep people here," Tart said. "The object is to help them move on."

Founder Ernie Mills agrees, as much as he laughs now at the obstacles he tried to put in Tart's way to start a thrift store.

"I had a belly full of thrift stores. When I first started, I worked for Neil Wilcox at the Winston-Salem Rescue Mission, and he worked me to death picking up furniture," Mills laughs. But, as he saw the financial stability and the jobs the Mission's Training Center offered, he came around and enthusiastically supported the thrift stores.

Kyle Drewry, now the training center manager, instructs clients on how to sort clothing to sell at the thrift stores.

"The income is nice, but the main thing I saw is it gives job training skills. A lot of our clients have been years and years without working in the workplace. The best way to get a job is if you have a job," Mills said, now a strong advocate of Tart's vision.

Co-founder Gail Mills said it's a blessing when they are out in the community and run into someone working in a retail setting who got their training at the Mission thrift stores.

"The thing about the thrift stores, I think it gives our clients hope. They see other clients that have been hired to work there. It builds them up that there is a job that they can do," she said.

∾

Faith Through the Choices, Crossroads and Roadblocks

∾

Crossing a road may seem trivial in the grand scheme of our lives, but as the Mission moves forward, it's a powerful and literal reminder of the choices that created the enduring legacy of the Durham Rescue Mission. Leaders walked that narrow path they were called to walk, relying on God's guidance. And throughout its history, what seemed like roadblocks were just a matter of timing in God's plan.

For a long time, the Mission was interested in a property directly across the street, but it just never seemed the right time or purpose. Rev. Rob Tart waited patiently as his vision grew for an expanded career development center that would be closer to the main Mission than the off-site Training Center. Instead of worrying over frustrating roadblocks and delays, he accepted things as they unfolded. But he made sure he was ready when the opportunity finally arose—just across the street.

One of the challenges of having the Mission Training Center off-site is transporting clients to and from campus and having to coordinate and deliver meals to the staff, Tart said.

In 2022, Tart saw the For Sale sign go up on parcel across the street and began inquiries. The $12 million price tag was not realistic for the Mission. Eventually he heard out-of-state investors had the property under contract, so he dropped the idea and began looking at other sites, letting the property owner know the Mission was pursuing a different nearby property instead.

Soon enough, the property owner came back to the Mission with a more affordable offer and dropped their out-of-state investor.

So, in December 2023, the Mission purchased a block of buildings directly across the street from the main campus adjacent to a smaller property they'd received through a donation from a non-profit organization.

By early 2024, Tart was ready with initial plans to build a new Mission training and career development center directly across the street from the Men's campus and main Mission building.

The Mission acquired an adjacent smaller parcel a decade or more before, on the condition that the Mission tear down the condemned building located there. The Mission considered a few ideas for the property since, but they never worked out. Now, combined with the new parcel, it provided enough land to plan a new training center right across from the Mission.

Most of the buildings on the property were vacant or uninhabitable—a few dilapidated houses, a couple small, closed warehouses, a former restaurant and a crumbling church that was once a house of worship to churches such as Peace Missionary Baptist Church and Liberty Baptist Church, vacant for years.

A career development and training center with modern classroom and storage space, along with a thrift store, would be a welcome improvement to the two city blocks previously in decades of decline, Tart surmised.

Despite structural issues, once the Mission had a contractor remove the asbestos in preparation for demolition of the old buildings, he did consider repurposing the abandoned old brick church into the new design. However, that May of 2024, a massive fire broke out and destroyed the church. Authorities were investigating the cause.

‿◌⁀

Crossing the Street: Trusting God's Plan for the Future

‿◌⁀

The Mission was developing its plans, including continuing to incorporate a large component of recycling into the process, which not only adds income but reduces trash costs through bulk sales of items that can be purchased and reused.

With a goal to break ground by the end of 2025, Tart expected to sell the original training center building to help fund the new construction, along with getting support from the Rescue Legacy Fund.

The vision for the new facility was to provide more opportunities for the Mission counseling staff to interact with the clients as they go about their daily training.

"It makes everything so much safer and so much more efficient," Tart said.

Stepping across the street also takes a leap of faith—trusting the Lord to lead the Mission further along its enduring road toward His purpose.

APPENDIX
Timeline

2006

The first Durham Rescue Mission Thrift Store opened at the corner of NC Highway 55 and Cornwallis Road in Durham, NC.

2007

L. Frederick Holloway, former client and current staff member, gets married.

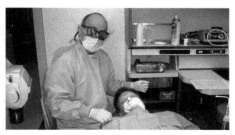

2009

The Samaritan Health Center opened a clinic at the Good Samaritan Inn for Durham Rescue Mission clients.

2009

The second Durham Rescue Mission Thrift Store opened on Glenwood Avenue in Raleigh, NC.

2010

Former Duke University head football coach David Cutcliffe brought his players to the Good Samaritan Inn to play with the children.

2012

Groundbreaking began the Center for Hope's construction located at the 1201 E. Main St. campus in Durham, NC

2013

Former NC governor Pat McCrory and former Durham mayor Bill Bell cut the ribbon to open the Center for Hope.

2013

A third thrift store opened on Chapel Hill Boulevard Durham, NC.

2015

The Durham Rescue Mission Job Training and Donation Center opened on S. Alston Avenue in Durham, NC.

2015

Renovations to the Durham Rescue Mission's Storr Office Chapel, including the installation of an elevator and a second stairwell, were made.

2017

The construction of the Ball Family Student Housing provided 64 more beds for the addicted and homeless.

2018

Ernie and Gail were each awarded the Order of the Long Leaf Pine, the highest honor awarded to citizens of North Carolina. Ernie celebrated his 50 years of service to the addicted and homeless.

2019

The new Clegg Family Student Housing added 54 beds for the addicted and homeless.

2019

The fourth Durham Rescue Mission Thrift Store opened in Wake Forest, NC

2021

Roxboro, NC, welcomed the opening of the fifth Durham Rescue Mission Thrift Store.

2022

Ernie Mills "passes the torch" of leadership of the Durham Rescue Mission to Rob Tart, who became Chief Executive Officer of the Mission in 2022.

2023

Named in honor of founders Ernie and Gail Mills, the new Mills Family Student Housing added 64 beds for the addicted and homeless.

2024

The largest Victory Program class in Durham Rescue Mission (57) graduated.

Printed in the USA
CPSIA information can be obtained
at www.ICGtesting.com
JSHW011521150924
69750JS00003BA/3